PERHAPS YOU TRULY CAN

Entrepre
MAC

WHY DO M

ARE YOU LIKE MOST A

EVERYBODY TALKS A

WHAT DO ALL ENTREPRENEURS HAVE IN

Get Smart!

365 TIPS TO BOOST YOUR ENTREPRENEURIAL

Rieva Lesonsky
Editorial Director, Entrepreneur Magazine

Other books by Rieva Lesonsky:

Start Your Own Business:
The Only Start-up Book You'll Ever Need

303 Marketing Tips
Guaranteed to Boost Your Business

Young Millionaires: Inspiring Stories to
Ignite Your Entrepreneurial Dreams

Entrepreneur MAGAZINE'S

Get Smart!

365 TIPS TO BOOST YOUR ENTREPRENEURIAL IQ

Rieva Lesonsky
Editorial Director, Entrepreneur Magazine

Entrepreneur Press
2392 Morse Ave., Irvine, CA 92614

Managing Editor: Marla Markman
Book Design: Cheryl K. Fujioki
Proofreader: Lynn Beresford
Cover Design: Mark A. Kozak
Indexer: Alta Indexing Service

This publication is designed to provide accurate and authoritative information in regard to the subject matter covered. It is sold with the understanding that the publisher is not engaged in rendering legal, accounting or other professional services. If legal advice or other expert assistance is required, the services of a competent professional person should be sought.

Library of Congress Cataloging-in-Publication Data

Lesonsky, Rieva.
        Get smart: 365 tips to boost your entrepreneurial IQ / by Rieva
Lesonsky.
            p.   cm.
        Includes index.
        ISBN 1-891984-09-8
        1. Success in business.   2. Entrepreneurship.   I. Title.
HF5386.L567   1999
658.4′21 —dc21   99-39749
                                                           CIP

Printed in Canada

09 08 07 06 05 04 03 02 01 00   10 9 8 7 6 5 4 3 2 1

To the small-business owners who shaped my past: my father, Jerry Lesonsky, my grandfathers, Jack Lesonsky and Harry Cash, and my uncles, Seymour Cash and Dave Cohen. And to you, the entrepreneurs who will shape my future.

ACKNOWLEDGMENTS

This book owes its existence to the persistence, creativity and peskiness of many. Thanks to *Entrepreneur* magazine's managing editor, Maria Valdez, and articles editors, Peggy Bennett and Janean Chun; *Entrepreneur's Business Start-Ups'* managing editor, Karen Axelton; the staff editors and writers and contributing writers of *Entrepreneur* and *Entrepreneur's Business Start-Ups'* magazines; the experts who shared their inside secrets; and Entrepreneur Press' managing editor, Marla Markman. Also thanks to Lee Jones, Carrie Fitzmaurice, Susan Stone Russell, Jim Huddleston and Anré Williams from American Express Small Business Services, Mark Gura, and especially Russ Monroe—this book wouldn't exist without you.

And to my schoolteachers: Henry Strickland, Fred Monner and James Alford; my work teachers: M.K. Ram, Peter Shea and Neil Perlman; and my life teachers: my parents, Mimi and Jerry Lesonsky, Maria Anton and Skip Brendmoen—thank you all for your faith and encouragement.

INTRODUCTION

I am a graduate of the University of Missouri's School of Journalism, which means nothing to most of you. Mizzou's J-school ranks among the top in the nation, and, indeed, I received a great education—in journalism. Why am I telling you this? Well, the problem is today I am more a manager than a journalist, and nobody taught me anything about that.

That's the same situation many entrepreneurs find themselves in. It's likely the business you started (or are about to launch) is one built around something you love, you know or you already do. So you come equipped with all the knowledge of your industry (OK, maybe not all) but know little about the rest of the "stuff." And that's what this book is all about—learning about all that other stuff, like management issues, raising money, marketing, hiring and firing people, taxes, time management, social responsibility, technological needs, health issues, balancing work and family, and so much more.

It's not just a matter of background and training. In today's fast-changing entrepreneurial world, it's hard to keep up. Like most entrepreneurs, you're so intent on growing your business, it's nearly impossible to stay on top of the latest tech innovations, management techniques and proven marketing methods. And entrepreneurs are notoriously short of time. So even if you had the inclination to study, you probably couldn't do it justice.

The format of this book should help. Here are 365 smart business tips to help you grow your businesses. Some will save you money; others will save you time. But, hopefully, you'll learn something from every one of them. The tips are short; each one takes up less than a page. You can use them like vitamins, and read one a day. Or you can ingest a few (or even many) at a time. It's totally up to you.

Problems and challenges crop up randomly in business; they do not come to us neatly grouped by category. And so this book purposely follows no formula. The tips are not arranged by topic or expertise level; rather, they are intended to help you tackle a problem you may be currently experiencing or plant a seed to help you solve a future concern.

Despite their brevity, these tips offer real solutions. My goal is to help you find the better, smarter, quicker fix. But, obviously, sometimes your problems require more than a quick fix. In these cases, a source for more information is cited. And whatever your situation or problem is, you can almost always learn more by checking out our Web sites at entrepreneurmag.com and biz startups.com.

I started my career at *Entrepreneur* back in 1978 when hardly anyone knew what an entrepreneur was, much less wanted to be one. It's quite a different world today—almost everyone is related to or knows an entrepreneur, and millions more annually aspire to entrepreneurship.

It's an exciting time for entrepreneurs: The world is clamoring for your quick thinking, your problem-solving, and your unique products and services. But it's hard to do it all, especially at the beginning when staff is short or nonexistent, when you have more questions than answers, and when there is never enough time in the day to run your business. But our philosophy at Entrepreneur Media Inc. is "No entrepreneur is ever alone—you have us."

So whether you check us out on the Web at entrepreneurmag.com; read our online e-zine, homeofficemag.com; read our print publications, *Entrepreneur, Entrepreneur's Business Start-Ups* or *Entrepreneur's Be Your Own Boss*; or buy our books, help is near. Our goal—in fact, our mission—is to help you start and grow your own business. Turn the page and find the knowledge and information that will make you a better and smarter entrepreneur and help you grow a bigger, more profitable business.

Business ownership is empowering. It will not necessarily give you the power to dominate the world or even your industry (although you never know) but rather the power to rule your own life. And what could be better than that?

Rieva Lesonsky

Rieva Lesonsky

VP/Editorial Director
Entrepreneur Media Inc.

P.S. If you have some smart tips of your own, let me know. Tell me how you solved your entrepreneurial problems. We'll publish some of the best tips in future issues of our publications. And if we use your tip, I'll send you a free copy of our booklet *37 Smart Ways to Manage Your Growing Business*. See the back of this book for more information and where to send your tips.

PERHAPS YOU TRULY CAN'T JUDGE A BOOK BY ITS COVER, BUT CONSUMERS CAN—AND DO— JUDGE A PRODUCT BY ITS PACKAGE.

And if you're trying to peddle your wares overseas, your packaging is even more crucial.

While what works in one country will not necessarily have the same effect in another, there are some universal truths:

Color is a package's most important element. Worldwide, red is generally considered a positive color, and gold usually signifies quality.

In Asia, packages should have an American and imported feel, and in Europe, you should go with an upscale, elegant look. Warm, bright colors connect in Latin America, and what sells in the United States works just as well in Canada.

Overseas, storage in homes and stores is an issue, so keep your packages small. Also, avoid clutter, and limit your use of numbers and words.

Most important: Do your homework! Remember, think globally, but act locally.

DO YOU SEND YOUR SALES LETTERS AND PROMOTIONAL MATERIALS IN A COMPANY ENVELOPE, EMBLAZONED WITH YOUR LOGO IN THE LEFT-HAND CORNER?

Most entrepreneurs do, and that can be a big mistake.

According to direct-mail guru Jerry Fisher, most people glance at their commercial mail and decide whether to toss or open it in a matter of seconds. Fisher claims you can save your mail from being trashed by sending it in a primarily blank envelope. Instead of spelling out your company's name in the return address, try creating an air of mystery and use only initials. For instance, here at Entrepreneur Press, we would send an envelope bearing only our return address, topped by the initials EP.

You might want to test your mailings, using one with an intriguing or compelling message printed on the envelope and one that's virtually blank. But mark Fisher's words: Sheer curiosity will get your "essentially anonymous" envelope opened more than 50 percent of the time.

That's why it's so important to choose your words with care.

EVERY TIME YOU SPEAK, YOU HAVE A CHANCE TO MAKE OR BREAK YOUR BUSINESS.

So says Donald Weiss, author of *Why Didn't I Say That?*, who suggests we eliminate the "ahs" and "uhs" from our vocabulary because they make us sound unsure and ill at ease.

Use active sentences, such as "We need to fix this now!" instead of the more passive "This is in need of some attention."

How we speak is just as important as what we say. Don't talk too loudly—or too fast. People are more apt to listen when spoken to in a relatively slow, lower tone of voice.

So be aware of how you sound. Powerful speech patterns can strengthen your image and influence.

And that could mean your business is headed for big trouble.

A recent study conducted by professors at UCLA and Stanford University showed most business owners are clueless when it comes to assessing their competition. Most of those surveyed misread their competitors' strategies, seeing reactions that simply did not occur. What's worse, almost 80 percent were blind to their opponents' actions, which can lead to losing both customers and market share.

But you can learn to keep up with your competition. Role play! Put yourself in their shoes, and analyze their strategies. Visit their stores, and use the Internet to dig up as much information as you can about them, their tactics and their goals.

Paying attention to the "little ones" may actually help your business grow.

"OUT OF THE MOUTHS OF BABES" IS MORE THAN JUST AN EXPRESSION.

If you're in the kids' business or considering starting one, you may want to consider using children as marketing consultants. Kids tend to think out of the box, and that can be an asset for entrepreneurs trying to reach this booming market.

Some companies give their young consultants regular homework assignments. And mega-enterprises like Microsoft and MTV regularly hire kids for their views.

But you don't need to make this such a formal process. Try polling the kids you know. Show them your stuff, ask what they think and then brainstorm with them. Don't be patronizing—you must be truly open to the process for it to work. And as we all know, "Kids say the darnedest things!"

CAN YOU STILL MAKE MONEY IN THE CROWDED MAIL ORDER FIELD?

Yes—if you follow these four steps to mail order success:

1. *Know your niche.* You should bring a special knowledge, insight or talent to your mail order specialty.
2. *Hit the books.* Immerse yourself in other companies' catalogs. Are they too long, too short? Do photos or illustrations work best? Make sure you also check out their order-processing methods.
3. *Find a list broker—fast.* Don't wait until you've printed your catalogs to pick your list broker. You need to incorporate the proper tracking codes, ensure your design is appropriate to your audience and print the right number of catalogs.
4. *Finally, know the code.* Make sure you take advantage of postal discounts.

Here's a bonus tip: Be patient; mail order empires are not built overnight.

DO YOUR MARKETING STRATEGIES NEED A BOOST?

Guerrilla marketing guru Jay Conrad Levinson offers these smart tips:

- Don't just network—build relationships. Send notes to people you've just met indicating you would like to talk again.
- Make sure your ads answer every consumer's No. 1 question: What's in it for me?
- Give something to your best customers. Gifts work best as a follow-up to a sale or a referral, on a holiday or for the customer's birthday.
- Personalize your faxes. And add an easy-response device, such as "To order, sign here and fax back."
- Know the best ways to reach a prospect. A letter followed by a phone call is tops. Next best is a referral, then a cold call.
- Always communicate with your customers, even when you're not trying to sell them anything. That's how you build relationships.

*But before you hire
a payroll service,
take these smart steps:*

Check out the service's reputation. Ask for references from clients, accountants and bankers.

Ask about the specific services available. Some companies help with payroll deductions and direct deposits.

Make sure the service knows about all the federal and state government requirements and regulations. Good services give you brochures to keep you informed.

Rates are based on your number of employees and how often they're paid. It costs more to handle weekly payrolls than biweekly ones.

Still hesitant? You can handle payroll yourself with special payroll software, but then it's your responsibility to keep up with changing regulations.

NO BUSINESS IS TOO SMALL TO USE A PAYROLL SERVICE. EVEN A COMPANY WITH FEWER THAN FIVE EMPLOYEES CAN BENEFIT FROM OUTSOURCING ITS PAYROLL.

Try incorporating "little acts of appreciation" into your daily business routine.

DO YOU TAKE THE TIME TO THANK YOUR EMPLOYEES? MOST ENTREPRENEURS, CONSUMED WITH GROWING THEIR BUSINESSES, DON'T DO IT OFTEN ENOUGH.

So says Rosalind Jeffries, author of *101 Recognition Secrets.*

For instance, instead of giving workers birthday cards at the office, why not mail them to their homes? Or after a job particularly well-done, handwrite or e-mail a congratulatory note. And make sure to give special recognition to employees who do good deeds in or out of the office.

Food treats can also serve as a general morale booster. Try serving hot chocolate on cold winter days or providing Popsicles to beat the summer swelter.

These gestures may sound trivial, but, as Jeffries reminds us, one of the greatest human needs is to be appreciated.

Instead, sales guru Danielle Kennedy suggests you reach out and touch as many people as you can.

I

Is YOUR BUSINESS RELYING ON ONLY ONE MARKET NICHE? IF SO, YOU COULD BE ASKING FOR TROUBLE.

If you're in a slump, the fastest way to jump-start your sales is to target past customers and ask them to refer you to their colleagues.

Or, when relevant, let your non-business acquaintances know what you do. Can you do business with someone at the gym or PTA? You'll never know if you don't ask.

Try forming your own board of advisors. Your lawyer, insurance agent or banker can supply you with good advice as well as a steady source of leads.

Or how about a blast from the past? Check out your old high school and college yearbooks, or contact people you used to work for or socialize with.

*Even if you sound like
Betty Boop or Elmer Fudd,
with awareness and practice,
you can develop an
effective speaking voice.*

Step one, says motivational speaker Don Abbott, is to breathe. And remember to pause every now and then.
If you talk nonstop, you'll sound anxious and insecure.

Don't forget to enunciate. And make sure your pronunciation is correct or you'll sound uneducated.

Pace yourself. Talking too slowly can be as ineffective as speaking too quickly.

If you're nervous, says Abbott, fess up! Tell the crowd you're a little uptight, and you'll put them— and yourself—at ease.

And remember, practice makes perfect. Once you get the drill down, you'll feel—and sound— more confident.

IT'S NOT ONLY WHAT YOU SAY BUT HOW YOU SAY IT THAT AFFECTS YOUR BUSINESS AND YOUR CREDIBILITY.

Well, experts say that may not be good enough.

Sure, every entrepreneur wants satisfied customers, but sales guru Danielle Kennedy believes you can—and should—do better than that: You can have loyal customers. What's the difference? Satisfied customers are still willing to listen to your competitors, but loyal clients think you're the greatest thing since someone sliced that proverbial bread.

You develop loyal customers by continually asking your satisfied ones if there's anything else you can do for them. And once you've got 'em, make them part of your sales team by asking them to refer you to their friends and colleagues.

But never stop courting your loyal customers; repeat customers should make up 75 percent of your clientele.

DO YOU HAVE COLLECTION PROTECTION?

Your ability to collect from past-due clients may depend on the language in your sales documents.

Have an attorney—preferably one who specializes in creditors' rights—review your documents, including credit applications, sales contracts, invoices and statements, to be sure they conform to your state's regulations. First up: Make sure your invoices state when the payment is due.

If you offer terms, you must clearly state the interest rate and conditions under which interest accrues. In some states, customers must agree to this in writing; find out if this applies to you. Also, stipulate that if there is a problem, the debtor is responsible for paying any attorney and collection fees.

Do yourself a favor: Protect yourself now and collections will be much easier later.

With the right precautions, though, anyone can take advantage of this great sales tool.

DO YOU OFFER GIFT CERTIFICATES TO YOUR CUSTOMERS? MANY ENTREPRENEURS DON'T BECAUSE THE POTENTIAL FOR FRAUD SCARES THEM.

- Don't buy generic gift certificates from stationery or office supply stores. These are too easily duplicated. Invest in custom-designed certificates.
- Avoid cash refunds. State on the certificate that if more than $5 worth of change is due, it will be issued as another certificate.
- Keep a log. Record the certificate number, date of sale and dollar amount. Make sure you note when the certificate is redeemed.
- Use security features like an embossed logo or watermark to prevent photocopying.
- Does this sound like a lot of trouble? It's really not, and certificates are a great way for you to expand your client base.

But there's an easy cure: Use a headset.

Headsets typically cost between $120 and $450, but headset manufacturer Hello Direct reports if you spend four hours a day on the phone, your increased productivity will make up the cost of the device in only 12 days.

When choosing a headset, consider your environment. If it's particularly noisy, you'll probably want a unit that covers both ears. Before you buy, determine how much weight you're comfortable with on your head.

Some folks don't like the feeling of a band around the top of their head. If you're one of them, buy a model that wraps around your ear.

And if you just can't sit still, consider a cordless unit. It not only frees up your hands—which increases productivity—but many people think more creatively while roaming around.

TALKING ON THE PHONE ONLY A FEW HOURS A DAY CAN BE A PAIN IN THE NECK FOR EVEN THE HEARTIEST ENTREPRENEURS.

Answer the following questions and find out.

Are you a tech company? Is your business capable of being a market leader? Do you have a clear distribution channel? How much will it take to build your business? Are your margins "fat" enough? And, finally, how fast can you grow?

Most venture capitalist invest in high-tech firms. And they rarely finance a company that is trying to take on a market leader (but they do make exceptions for businesses capable of producing breakthrough technologies).

Give yourself a big plus if you've got a clear and easy way to sell your product or service. You're also looking golden if your business can be built for less than $10 million, will generate margins of 50 percent and can grow to $25 million in five years.

Doesn't sound like you? Don't fret. There are more places than ever for entrepreneurs to seek funding. All it takes is a little home-work—and a lot of determination.

EVERY ENTREPRENEUR DREAMS ABOUT FINDING VENTURE CAPITAL. BUT MOST DON'T EVER GET IT. DO YOU HAVE A SHOT?

I BET YOU THINK INVOICES AND BILLING STATEMENTS EXIST ONLY TO HELP YOU COLLECT MONEY.

Well, you're wrong. They can help you grow your business, too.

Why not turn your invoices into marketing communications tools? Since you have to send out invoices anyway, use them to your advantage.

On your invoices, try adding computer-generated messages to your invoices promoting upcoming events, new products or services, or seasonal announcements. Plan your invoice messages three months in advance so you can promote different events and programs during each billing cycle.

Printing directly on the invoice ensures your messages get read. This simple act enables your customers to understand more about your company and how they can more effectively do business with you.

ARE YOU A
PARANOID
BUSINESS
OWNER? IF NOT,
PERHAPS YOU
SHOULD LEARN
TO BE.

Paranoia can be a key to your entrepreneurial success.

No, I'm not pulling your leg. Ask Andy Grove, founder of computer chip giant Intel.

Grove says you're paranoid if you pay attention to the details of your business, realize that others envy your success and watch for the trouble that inevitably occurs. Simply put: Paranoid entrepreneurs don't get complacent or rest on their laurels.

Grove so believes in the power of paranoia, he wrote a book called *Only the Paranoid Survive.* Paranoia, he says, helps keep business owners knee-deep in the details of their businesses.

If you're paranoid, it means you're sweating the small stuff. But that's OK. Smart entrepreneurs have turned worrying into an art form. Just don't get so lost in the details that you lose sight of the big picture.

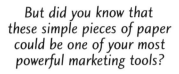

*But did you know that
these simple pieces of paper
could be one of your most
powerful marketing tools?*

ALL OF US HAVE
CLIPPED
COUPONS AT
ONE TIME OR
ANOTHER.

Coupons are merely incentives to do business with you. But with them, you can achieve several goals. Are you introducing a new product or service? Do you need to increase your repeat business? Coupons help you do both, as well as help fend off competitors, re-inforce a current ad campaign or even soften the blow of a price increase.

Direct mail is not your only choice for distribution. Consider running coupons in local news-papers or even on the Internet.

Remember, coupons are more than just words on pieces of paper. Be sure your coupons are clear, stating precisely what the offer is, how long it lasts and how cus-tomers can redeem them. And get ready: Most entrepreneurs report that coupons increase business significantly.

Here are some ground rules to help keep you out of trouble:

- Don't touch your employees without permission.
- Don't treat employees as potential dates, and whatever you do, never get involved with someone who works for you.
- Don't demean others, especially in reference to their gender.
- Don't make suggestive comments.
- Watch your language; what amuses some can offend others.
- Make sure your company has a written sexual harassment policy and that all employees know what to do if they're harassed.
- Take all complaints seriously, and launch an immediate investigation.

ARE YOU SAFE FROM SEXUAL HARASSMENT CHARGES? YOU MAY THINK YOU ARE, BUT THESE DAYS BUSINESS OWNERS CAN'T BE TOO CAREFUL.

You have to worry about more than yourself. Make sure your employees are not harassing each other, either. But remember, it's your business—and you set the tone.

You have to learn how to network the right way.

First, develop a plan. Networking is more than just saying hello. It's the smart way to build long-lasting business relationships.

Decide who your best prospects are and where you're likely to find them. Then go where they are: committees, conferences, meetings or associations.

Learn to make small talk. Ask open-ended questions. And don't forget to listen.

Don't think of networking as just a sales opportunity. Instead, consider it a mission—a chance to learn something. The sales will come later.

Always follow up. If you don't, you've wasted your time, not to mention your energy and money. Most important, be prepared. Networking opportunities can—and do—crop up unexpectedly.

ARE YOU A NETWORKING NERD? MANY CONSIDER NETWORKING SO SIMPLE ANYONE CAN DO IT, BUT DON'T LISTEN TO THEM.

ARE YOUR
BUSINESS
INSURANCE
COSTS OUT OF
CONTROL?

*You can keep your expenses
down if you practice these
good insurance habits.*

Review your insurance needs and
coverage annually. If your business
is growing rapidly, you might want
to check it more frequently.

Ask your insurance agent to help
you reduce your risks. Have him or
her visit your premises and point
out where you can make improvements.

Check out new insurance products. Make sure your agent keeps
you up to date on any new types of
coverage you may need.

No business is too new—or too
small—for insurance. And if you're
homebased and think your homeowner's insurance is adequate,
you're likely in for a big, unpleasant
surprise.

Like the old song says "You better shop around." Sure, you're busy.
But a few hours of research now
can save you thousands of dollars
in premiums or claims later.

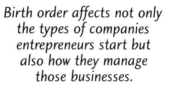

Birth order affects not only the types of companies entrepreneurs start but also how they manage those businesses.

DID YOU KNOW THAT WHETHER YOU'RE THE OLDEST OR YOUNGEST IN YOUR FAMILY INFLUENCES HOW YOU RUN YOUR BUSINESS?

That's according to a recent study conducted by Frank Sulloway for his book *Born to Rebel*.

Sulloway says first-borns tend to be conscientious, obedient, hard-driving and bossy. Later-borns are more flexible, innovative, laid-back and sociable. These characteristics can impact entrepreneurs from the start: Older siblings often go for the safe bet, while the younger ones are likely to be risk takers. First-borns might make better franchisees, while later-borns often undertake more experimental and quirkier businesses.

The solution? Sulloway suggests, if possible, join forces with your siblings. Together, you offset your "inborn weaknesses" and can build a better business.

ARE YOU A
GOOD BOSS?
YOU MAY
THINK SO, BUT
HOW DO YOU
REALLY KNOW?

*One way is to
compare yourself to
other bosses.*

A good place to start is Jim Miller's book *Best Boss, Worst Boss*.

Since many business owners are unaware of their behavior, Miller hopes that reading good boss, bad boss stories can teach you to be one of the good ones. If, for example, you're like the tightwad owner who charges his staff 30 cents for every personal phone call, you'll likely have a harder time attracting employees.

Being a "good" entrepreneur often directly impacts the bottom line. Miller's best bosses are generous, empowering and compassionate. And workers who feel appreciated are not only happier but more productive, efficient and loyal, which can only help your business grow.

Today's technology has made it easier than ever for crooks to commit check fraud.

More than 1 million bad checks enter the banking system every day.

But you can protect your business; here's how:

- Store your checks in a secure area.
- Track check numbers so you'll notice missing checks.
- Evaluate your check-issuing process, and conduct an audit to detect any risk areas.
- Everyone hates to do it, but you must reconcile your bank statements as soon as possible.
- Add several security features to your checks. Your checks should indicate that they're protected, and you should inform your bank of the security measures you've taken. If the bank pays a check that doesn't include your security features, you are not responsible for the loss.

IT'S 10 O'CLOCK. DO YOU KNOW WHERE YOUR CHECKS ARE— OR ARE FORGERS MAKING A FORTUNE OFF OF YOU?

IQ25

But you can learn how to protect your business.

Telemarketing scam artists sell overpriced, poor-quality office goods to unsuspecting entrepreneurs.

The Federal Trade Commission requires telemarketers to disclose certain information, including that it's a sales call, who they are, and the total cost of the goods or services they're selling. So don't be afraid to ask.

Keep track of all orders. And limit the number of staff members who are authorized to order items. If you receive merchandise you did not order—and the seller cannot prove you did—you can keep the materials.

Make sure your employees are scam-aware and establish a procedure for taking and handling such calls. Remember, forewarned is forearmed.

WATCH OUT! YOU'RE AN EASY TARGET FOR ONE OF THE MOST COMMON—AND MOST COSTLY— BUSINESS SCAMS.

HUNTING
FOR AN
INSURANCE
AGENT?
DON'T GO
INTO THE
SEARCH
UNARMED.

*Before you sign on the
dotted line, ask your agent
for some answers.*

How long has the agency been
around? If it's new, find out if the
principals have extensive industry
experience.

Is the agent familiar with your
industry? What is his or her background, experience and education?

Does the agent actually listen to
you and address your concerns, or
do you feel like you're getting a
cookie-cutter presentation?

Will you be "just a client?"
Clients get sold insurance. Instead
look for an agent who wants to be
your partner—one who helps you
analyze your risks.

Check references. Sure, that's
obvious, but busy entrepreneurs
frequently don't bother.

How comfortable do you feel?
Remember you are entrusting this
person with the future of your business.

*Follow these tips to
make sure your money is
working as hard as you are.*

- *Are you saving enough money?*
  Start building your nest egg now
  by saving at least 10 percent of
  your annual income.
- *Do you have an IRA, a 401(k)
  or SEP plan?* If not, start one
  today.
- *Where are your investments?*
  Don't put all your eggs in one
  basket. Make sure your investments are diversified.
- *Do you know where your money
  goes?* For one month, keep close
  track of how you spend your
  money. You'll be amazed by what
  you uncover.
- *Are you prepared for life's big
  events?* School costs, a new
  house, a wedding? You need a
  targeted savings plan for these
  circumstances.

Most important, find a financial
advisor you like and trust. Ask for
their advice—and follow it!

CHANCES ARE
YOU'RE GOING
TO LIVE
A GOOD,
LONG LIFE.
BUT ARE YOU
FINANCIALLY
PREPARED
FOR IT?

THERE'S A BIG DIFFERENCE BETWEEN PLEASING YOUR CUSTOMERS AND ASTONISHING THEM.

If you want to dazzle your clients, listen up!

- *Go out of your way for loyal customers.* Do them a favor: Locate a hard-to find item or, if your staff is tied up, do the work yourself.
- *Underpromise and overdeliver.* Do they need it in two weeks? Give it to them in one.
- *Offer your best customers a benefit they didn't even know existed.* Did they miss your coupon in the paper? Give them the discount anyway.
- *Follow up, especially after a big order or a major project.* Are they satisfied, or is there something else you can do for them?
- *Above all, be honest.* Don't oversell goods or services. Show them you have their best interests at heart, and you'll have a customer for life.

HOMEBASED ENTREPRENEURS OFTEN HAVE A TOUGH TIME GROWING THEIR BUSINESSES BECAUSE THEY HAVE TO GO IT ALONE.

So we asked some successful homebased business owners to share their best advice.

- *Be a good neighbor.* Make sure your neighbors know what you're doing and that it won't impact them negatively.
- *Work hard to balance home and work.* This is hard for all entrepreneurs, but it's particularly difficult if you work and live in the same place.
- *Be patient.* There are few true overnight successes. Make a plan, and stick with it.
- *Go that extra mile.* Finding customers can be harder if you're homebased. So make sure you please the ones you have each and every time.
- *Finally, get out of the house!* Meet your friends or former colleagues for lunch. Join a group or association, or form an informal advisory board.

ARE THE WALLS CLOSING IN ON YOU?

Then maybe it's time to move to a bigger space.

Heed this advice on searching for new digs from Jack Gold, president of Sterling Management, a relocation consulting company:

- *Figure out how much space you really need.* Don't guess; miscalculations can be costly.
- *Establish a budget.* And don't forget to include relocation expenses in your plan.
- *Check out the building's power supply.* Older structures may not have enough power for today's equipment-laden businesses.
- *Ask about the office's services and access.* Can you get in 24 hours a day, seven days a week? Is the building heated or cooled at night or on the weekends?

If all this sounds like too much for you to handle, consider hiring a consultant to do the legwork for you.

The key?
Constant communication.

DOES YOUR COMPANY USE INDEPENDENT CONTRACTORS? MANY SMALL BUSINESSES DO BUT HAVE DIFFICULTY RETAINING THEM.

Independent contractors who feel like they're part of your business work harder for you. To make sure they keep up, send memos or hold meetings with your independent contractors so they know how vital they are to you.

Offer additional training if necessary, and try to include independent contractors in your company's holiday parties and other social events.

But remember, you must maintain the line between employees and independent contractors. If they are not truly independent—and you can get a free checklist from your local IRS office to make sure—you are risking violating numerous tax laws.

*But first, give up the idea
that you must
come out the winner.*

WINNING AT
NEGOTIATIONS
MAY BE SIMPLER
THAN YOU
THINK.

That's the advice of Ron
Shapiro, sports agent for legendary
baseball stars like Cal Ripken.

Shapiro believes successful
negotiators leave both sides happy
and use the process to build future
relationships. If you try for a win-
lose scenario, Shapiro says, you'll
end up with a case of lose-lose.
Instead, go for a win-win situation.

Shapiro teaches a 3-P negotiating strategy: Prepare, probe and
propose. Entrepreneurs, he claims,
often have trouble with the preparation and the probing, simply
because they talk too much and
don't listen.

So next time you're negotiating,
take Shapiro's advice: "Get all you
can, but also try to accommodate
the other side's needs."

IT'S INBRED— MOST CONSUMERS ARE SKEPTICAL. SO IT'S YOUR JOB TO CONVINCE YOUR CUSTOMERS THAT THEY NEED YOUR PRODUCT OR SERVICE.

How? Try these pointers:

- *Acknowledge the customer's fears.* Telling them not to worry is not enough; you have to directly address their fears.
- *Ask questions.* Too many entrepreneurs believe the customer will think this a waste of time, but you can't soothe their worries if you don't know what they are.
- *Promise to follow up.* And make sure you keep that promise. Find out how the customer would like you to stay in touch—by phone, letter or a face-to-face meeting.
- *Emphasize value.* Many consumers fear being overcharged. Combat this by stressing the value of your product or service.
- *Most important, communicate.* The key to serving your customers well is to meet their expectations.

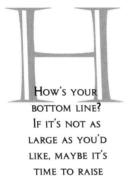

One of the easiest ways to increase profits is to boost prices.

How's your bottom line? If it's not as large as you'd like, maybe it's time to raise prices.

But don't initiate an immediate across-the-board price hike. Instead, use a niche-pricing technique: Find the areas within your business where you can support an increase. Price is based on perceived value, so you have to find the places where you are undervaluing your product or service.

To do this, study costs—yours and your competitors'. Then analyze your competitive advantages and disadvantages. This is not an easy process, but it's well worth the effort. Once you identify the areas where you've undervalued your product or service, adjust those prices accordingly. Make sure you give your customers advance notice, explain the increase and focus on value, not price.

If you're serious about growing your business, it may be time to think about a loan.

Bankers and other financial advisors say there are four crucial times when small businesses should seek a loan:

- When it's time to hire new employees,
- When you're trying to increase long-term sales,
- When you want to increase your market share, and
- When you'd like to take advantage of suppliers' early payment discounts.

If this sounds like you, or if you simply need money to pay bills, pay off creditors or improve cash flow, a loan may be your answer. But it's important not to take on too much debt. Check with your financial advisors to make sure you're not taking on more than you can handle.

SOME ENTREPRENEURS HAVE NEVER BORROWED A DIME, AND BELIEVE IT OR NOT, THAT CAN HINDER YOUR BUSINESS'S GROWTH.

Learning to speak effectively can only boost your business.

ARE YOU LIKE MOST AMERICANS, WHO RANK PUBLIC SPEAKING AS THEIR GREATEST FEAR? WELL, GET OVER IT!

Step one is to promote yourself as an expert in your field. Start out speaking to business and civic groups. Volunteer to speak at a conference or industry trade show, or offer free seminars. The key is to get experience speaking in front of groups of people.

Once you get the opportunity to speak in public, make sure you do it well. Preparation is key. Know your audience; it helps you personalize your message. Don't ramble; make sure you organize your thoughts. And rehearse, rehearse, rehearse. Practice does make perfect.

Not sure why you should do this? Once you fine-tune your public speaking, you'll be better at conducting meetings, making sales presentations and negotiating with clients, suppliers and bankers.

But not having a will is one of the biggest mistakes small-business owners make.

DO YOU HAVE A WILL? IF YOU'RE LIKE MOST ENTREPRENEURS, THE ANSWER IS NO.

No matter your age or the size of your business, you can't afford to put off writing your will.

In your will, you'll need to specify whom you want to run your company and name your beneficiaries. It's also important to understand the basics of estate planning and taxes. Books and software are available to help you draft your will. But before you finalize the document, make sure you review it with an estate attorney.

Still not convinced you need a will? Think about this: If something were to happen to you, your business could be in for a bumpy transition, and your family could lose everything you've worked so hard to build.

Misguided entrepreneurs believe once they've made the sale, they can stop their marketing efforts.

"Wrong," says Levinson. That's when marketing should begin.

Follow-up is essential to keeping customers. Here's an abbreviated version of Levinson's follow-up calendar: Within two days of making the sale, send your customers a thank-you note. Thirty days later, send another note or call to find out if the customer has any questions. Within 90 days, send buyers another note, telling them about related products or services. After nine months, ask for the names of three people you can add to your mailing list. On the one-year anniversary of the sale, send a card, perhaps with a discount included.

Sound like a lot of trouble? Consider this: According to Levinson, it costs six times more to sell something to a new customer than to an existing one.

Though we all hope it never happens, someday you may have to file an insurance claim. Do you know what to do?

Here are some tips that may ease the process:

- Immediately report any incidents—accidents, theft, fire or other damage—to your agent or insurance carrier.
- Make sure you protect your property from further damage; temporary repairs are covered in most policies.
- If possible, save any damaged property. Your claims adjuster may want to see it.
- Most policies ask for at least two repair estimates; find out what kind of estimate documentation your carrier requires.
- The insurance company needs proof of loss, so document everything, including financial data before and after the incident.
- Most important? Keep your agent informed. You never know when you'll need his or her help.

WHAT DO YOU DO WHEN BUSINESS IS BOOMING, BUT YOU DON'T HAVE THE CASH TO MEET THE DEMAND AND YOU CAN'T GET A LOAN?

Try factoring.

This is a process in which you sell—for cash—your accounts receivable to a third party.

The factor pays you about 75 percent of the invoiced amount upfront and delivers the rest—minus his or her fee—when paid by your client. Generally, the factor keeps about 6 percent of the invoice.

Since factors are more concerned about your client's ability to pay than yours, you may be able to factor even when you can't qualify for a loan. Small businesses often turn to factoring to fund growth or take advantage of early-payment discounts.

Look for factors in the phone book, or get a recommendation from your banker or financial advisor. Remember, though, factoring is a short-term solution. Most companies use this method for two years or less as they transition to more traditional types of financing.

HIDDEN CAMERAS CAN DO MORE THAN PROVIDE LAUGHS. VIDEO CAN BE AN EFFECTIVE MEANS OF LOSS CONTROL FOR ENTREPRENEURS.

And today video surveillance is increasingly affordable.

Companies use video cameras to detect—and deter—crimes committed by outsiders as well as employees. They can also be used to resolve workplace disputes, customer complaints and negligence charges.

Before you make a decision, you'll probably want to consult with several security vendors. You'll also need to decide whether to hide your camera or keep it in view. And make sure you set up a tape storage system so you can review tapes if necessary.

Remember, a camera will initially make your employees nervous. So make sure you assure your workers that none of them are under suspicion. Explain that the system is for everyone's protection.

*And it's not necessarily
a positive attribute.*

ALTHOUGH MANY ENTREPRENEURS MAY NOT WANT TO HEAR THIS, APPARENTLY THERE IS SUCH A THING AS AN ENTREPRENEURIAL PERSONALITY.

Although the characteristics small-business owners share often help them get their companies off the ground, these traits can also stand in the way of success.

For instance, entrepreneurs tend to be task-focused, which can make them less-than-sympathetic bosses. And while entrepreneurs are usually visionaries, they aren't particularly adept at communicating that vision. The strong personality of the entrepreneur can create another problem—others are often too cowed to disagree.

So can an entrepreneur change his or her spots? Obviously, awareness of how you come across to others—especially your employees—is vital. And realize that as you grow, you'll probably need to be a bit more deliberate and a little less seat-of-the-pants.

In his book, Success Secrets of the Motivational Superstars, *Michael Jeffreys tells how you, too, can achieve your goals.*

YOU CAN LEARN A LOT FROM THE SUCCESS OF OTHERS.

- *Do not be or act like a victim.* Realize that much of what happens is within your control, and take 100 percent responsibility for your life.
- *Get a sense of purpose.* That leads to loving what you do and a desire to do it right.
- *Be willing to pay the price.* Success does not come cheap or easily; you have to work—and work hard—to achieve it.
- *Stay focused.* This is harder than it sounds. Entrepreneurs are always pulled in various directions. Vow to spend part of the day focusing on your goals.
- *Be a copycat.* The quickest way to become successful is to find out what the best are doing, apply it to your situation and then do what they do.

Before you take on the costs and hassle of hiring permanent employees, consider these alternatives.

THINK YOU'RE READY TO HIRE YOUR FIRST EMPLOYEE?

If your need is seasonal or project-based, consider hiring temporary employees from a service. While temps might cost more on an hourly basis, in the long run, you'll save time, energy and money.

Independent contractors are another good source of help. But be careful here. This is a hot area for the IRS. Make sure your independent contractors are truly independent. Not sure? Contact the IRS for a free booklet.

Or consider college students; they often work for free or low wages if they can earn class credit. Ask local colleges if they have an internship program you can participate in. Remember, full-time employees cost more than just their wages. Before you hire, make sure you truly have to.

*Sure, that's great,
but that doesn't mean
women entrepreneurs
can get complacent.*

IN THE PAST
10 YEARS,
THE NATION'S
ENTREPRENEURIAL
WOMEN HAVE
GROWN THEIR
BUSINESSES TO
RECORD NUMBERS.

If you've been spending the past few years growing your business, now may be a good time to do some self-assessment.

A recent study showed that most entrepreneurial women are proficient at meeting deadlines, recognizing trends, resolving conflicts, adapting to change and generating new ideas. How do you rank at these tasks? Is there a specific area you need to work on?

The study also revealed most entrepreneurial women are not very good at coping with frustration or handling pressure. Does this sound like you?

No matter how successful you are, it's important to identify your weak points so you can strengthen them.

No matter what stage your business is in, one thing's for sure: money matters.

Here are some money-saving ideas to boost your business's bottom line:

- Cut your advertising costs by piggybacking your ad materials with other mailings, including invoices, reminder notices and thank-you notes.
- If you wait until the last minute, you can often buy cheaper ad space in local newspapers and magazines.
- You can fax for less by not using a cover sheet, sending faxes in the standard rather than fine mode, and waiting until the rates go down to transmit.
- Market research needn't be pricey. Set up a suggestion box for your customers to use, and get their names and addresses for your mailing list.

*Follow these tips to stay
up to date—and on budget:*

TECHNOLOGY
DOESN'T HAVE
TO BREAK YOUR
WALLET.

Are you taking advantage of
e-mail? Using e-mail can cut down
on your copier, overnight and
postal fees.

How Internet-savvy are you?
Advertising on the Web can cost
less than other mediums—just
make sure your targeted audience is
online as well. Create your own
Web site, and save the thousands it
would cost to outsource the job.
Place ads on someone else's site
and link your site to theirs to reach
a larger audience.

Or contact one of the cyber
malls, which can help you set up a
page on their site for very little
money. And don't overlook the
freeware and low-cost shareware
available at many online software
stores.

LET'S TALK
ABOUT BILLS—
SPECIFICALLY,
YOUR UTILITY
BILLS.

*Sure you're busy;
what entrepreneur isn't?
But make the time
to check your bills.*

Your phone bill is a good place to start. Before you dial a vendor, a supplier or even a customer, check the toll-free directory to see if the company has a toll-free number. Shop all the local and long-distance phone companies for the best deal. Cellular phone bills are often riddled with errors. Make sure you're charged only for calls that you made and ones that actually went through.

You can lower your electricity bills as well. Turn off machines when they're not in use. And use fluorescent lights; they not only conserve energy but also cost less to use. Today, many utility companies offer special rates to small businesses. Call yours to find out if you qualify.

Every entrepreneur needs insurance, but not everyone can afford it.

Here's how to keep a lid on insurance costs:

- When shopping for insurance, make sure you contact your trade association. Many offer discounted group rates to their members.
- Don't automatically renew your policies. Periodically check your needs, and always get several bids before renewing.
- Many entrepreneurs scrimp on disaster coverage—don't! Make sure you're protected, or you could lose your business.
- Consider raising your deductibles. Usually, this lowers premiums.
- Check your workers' comp insurance classification rate to make sure you're getting the proper discount.
- Sponsor a wellness program for your workers. Healthy employees can cut your health-claim costs significantly.

Try these money-saving tips:

Being an entrepreneurial road warrior doesn't have to cost you a fortune.

When calling from a hotel or pay phone, ask about charges. If they're too high, ask to be connected to your regular long-distance carrier. If you use a charge card to call from hotels, don't hang up between calls. Just press the pound key and dial the next call without re-entering your account number. This avoids the connect surcharges many hotels charge.

Also, you should always shop around for the best rates on hotel rooms. And make sure to ask about any discounts or specials. The same goes for car rentals. And don't pay for collision coverage if you don't have to. Check your credit card agreement; many include car rental insurance if you use that card to rent the car.

Instead, think of mail order as another method of selling your products.

YOU DON'T
HAVE TO BE IN
THE MAIL
ORDER BUSINESS
TO MAKE
MONEY FROM
MAIL ORDER.

The National Mail Order Association reminds us that adding a mail order component to your business doesn't have to be a complicated process. First, develop a database of your existing customers. This not only starts your mailing list, but should give you a clue about which bestselling items to include in your initial mailing.

When it comes to catalogs, it's smart to start small. Test a few products in a simple, basic catalog. Later, you can move up to a snazzier piece with more items in it.

Remember, mail order is not an inexpensive business. You might need to expand your facilities or hire more workers. Make sure you're prepared to spend some money, but it should be worth it.

*But free gifts can be
great marketing tools.*

Do you bribe your customers? You might quickly answer "Of course not."

Free gifts like a T-shirt, caps, coffee mugs, scratch pads and mouse pads can be really effective. Giving these away can generate leads, boost store traffic and increase awareness of your business.

When considering free gifts, first figure out whom you want to reach and how much money you have to spend. Then focus on the gift and the message you want to print on it.

Are freebies worth it? Experts say 40 percent of recipients remember the name of the company that sent the gift and about one-third still use the gift six months later. And best yet, free gifts can increase your average order by 300 percent.

*Providing good service
is the fastest, least expensive
way to make more money.*

Entrepreneurs are in a great position to take advantage of this.

Start by satisfying your customers the minute they walk through your door. Remember, they're busy, so take care of them as quickly as possible. Then really listen to them: Find out what they want and when they need it. As the boss, it's your responsibility to instill the right customer service attitude in all your employees, even part-timers. Training and appreciation will help your workers get it right.

Is it worth it? You bet it is! Customer service is a small investment that ultimately brings a lot of business.

EVERYBODY TALKS ABOUT CUSTOMER SERVICE, BUT HOW MANY ACTUALLY DO SOMETHING ABOUT IT?

A LOT HAS BEEN SAID ABOUT HOW EMPOWERING EMPLOYEES CAN HELP BUSINESSES GROW.

But what is it really all about?

Empowerment is merely giving your staff the authority to make decisions like letting them hire new employees and rewarding them for making great choices. This is especially hard for entrepreneurs, who often have difficulty delegating any task and incorrectly believe only they are capable of making the right call. Empowerment is popular with workers. It not only boosts job satisfaction, but it also reduces absenteeism and creates job loyalty, which decreases job turnover and improves customer service. That alone will save you money. Finally, it also frees you up to do what you do best . . . all of which can end up giving your business a strong competitive advantage.

Well, predicting trends isn't necessarily as hard as it appears.

DON'T WE ALL WISH WE HAD INSIGHT SO WE COULD BETTER GROW OUR BUSINESSES?

First, look to yourself, your friends, family and colleagues. What grabs your attention will likely captivate others as well. Are you spending more time in the garden? Dressing more casually? Or ordering more by mail? These are all clues.

Next, look around you. What are Americans watching on TV? What are the most popular movies? Reading magazines and newspapers—and not just your local ones—often leads to insights you can build ideas on.

Futurist Watts Wacker says you can hone your predictive skills by merely listening more, especially to people whose points of view are different than yours. What could be more simple? Paying attention really works.

*Being a subcontractor
or regular supplier to a
big business can really boost
your bottom line.*

But before you go knocking on doors, heed these tips:

DID YOU KNOW ONE OF THE SMARTEST WAYS FOR SMALL BUSINESSES TO GROW IS TO TEAM UP WITH CORPORATE GIANTS?

- Look at your track record. Many of the big guys shy away from start-ups and expect you to be in business for about five years. Your experience should also reflect an upscaling of your client base.
- Make sure you have references.
- Be sure you are capable of fulfilling what you say you can. If you mess up once, you may not get another chance.
- Work on building a solid financial base so you don't run short of cash.

Don't start by trying to determine what a big business might need. Instead, define what you can offer a big business and then find a company that needs what you can offer.

*So let's take the time
to give your business
an image checkup.*

FIRST
IMPRESSIONS
ARE IMPORTANT
FOR BUSINESSES,
BUT MANY
ENTREPRENEURS
DON'T BOTHER
TO CHECK
THEIRS.

First, if you have a sign, take a look at it. Does it grab attention and convey a sense of quality and stability? Does it say too much . . . or not enough?

Remember, neatness counts. How crowded are your display shelves? If you have plants, make sure they're green and healthy. Are your brochures and other literature relevant and current?

How's your packaging? This includes bags, envelopes, stationery and business cards. Is your logo up-to-date and professional-looking? Are your mailings clear and concise? Check your paper and printing as well as your message.

Don't put this off. Check your business image sometime this month and once a year thereafter.

A PICTURE
INDEED
CAN BE WORTH
A THOUSAND
WORDS.

*Remember this when planning
your advertising materials.*

Do you concentrate your energies on the words and ignore the visuals? That could be a big mistake.

To today's overloaded consumer, ads must be more than a diversion. They need to have the power to stop people in their tracks. To do this, you need all the elements working for you. But most important is a strong headline and an unusual or unique visual. Many entrepreneurs work hard on their headlines but too often believe a pretty or nice visual will do. The visual must be truly arresting or your ad will simply not get read.

Not convinced? Think of all the attention the milk folks have garnered with their milk mustache ads. See? Visuals work.

*They all have birthdays.
And their happy occasions
can mean more business for you.*

WHAT'S THE
ONE THING ALL
YOUR
CUSTOMERS
HAVE IN
COMMON?

How? By giving your customers birthday freebies. For instance, restaurant owners can give away a free meal. Shop owners can give away a gift or offer a discount. Salon owners can offer a free manicure or conditioning treatment. The idea is to make the customer feel important and become loyal to your business. And since it costs a lot less to retain old customers than to land new ones, this simple personalized gesture can actually save and make you money.

It's easy to keep track of customers' birthdays. Create your own simple database or hire a consultant to help. However you approach it, celebrating your customers' birthdays can bring you many happy returns.

Watts Wacker, co-author of The 500-Year Delta: What Happens After What Comes Next, *says every business needs one.*

T

But since most of us cannot even conceive of planning 500 years into the future, you might want to think of it as developing a long-term plan.

Simply ask yourself what your company promises and what it stands for. If you can answer that and keep your promises, Wacker says you're 70 percent of the way to success. Wacker studied long-standing businesses and discovered some common traits. They had access to money and a willingness to try new things. Most important, none of the companies still make money from the businesses they were originally in. How did they adapt and thrive? Wacker says it's simple: They created a long-term plan and followed it. And you can do it, too.

Is "SOCIALLY RESPONSIBLE BUSINESS" AN OXYMORON? No!

Entrepreneurs can do good and make profits, too.

Make social responsibility an important part of your marketing message. Sixty percent of customers will actually switch retail loyalties if the store is involved in a good cause. Pick a cause relevant to your customers. For instance, a book chain in Texas promotes literacy. Restaurant owners have banded together to fight hunger.

Remember to involve your customers, too. If they donate a used item, you can give them a discount on a new one.

And be prepared to say no. Once the word gets out about your charitable efforts, you'll likely get many requests for help, but it's better to do one project very well than to spread yourself too thin. Remember, it's a win-win situation. You win, but so does your community.

SURE, EVERYONE'S TALKING ABOUT GOING GLOBAL, BUT CAN ENTREPRENEURS ACTUALLY DO IT?

Yes. Here's how:
First, do your homework.

There's tons of free information out there. Start by contacting the Department of Commerce. Develop an international pricing strategy, taking fluctuating foreign currencies into account. And know upfront how you will be paid.

Learn the laws—all of them. This includes the U.S. regulations as well as the ones of the nations where you will be doing business. Look for opportunities everywhere, not just in the countries you learned about in school.

Also, remember, entrepreneurship is hot worldwide. Global entrepreneurs are looking for you as well. There's a lot of value in the words "Made in America."

The solution? Find a mentor.

Start your search for a mentor by thinking about all the successful people you know. Next, figure out what you expect from a mentor. A mentor should:

I

IT'S NEVER
EASY GOING
IT ALONE,
BUT START-UP
ENTREPRENEURS
MAY FIND IT
PARTICULARLY
HARD FLYING
SOLO.

- *have your best interests at heart.* You should feel free to share sensitive information with your mentor and be confident, he or she won't betray your trust.
- *speak honestly.* You don't need someone who is worried about sparing your feelings. A mentor should be able to objectively tell you what he or she thinks
- *get to know you.* A mentor does you no good if he or she is not aware of your skills and talents. A good mentor should also have a solid working knowledge of your industry.

Most important, listen to your mentor. If you don't follow your mentor's advice, chances are he or she is not going to be mentoring you for much longer.

How you HANDLE CUSTOMER COMPLAINTS CAN MAKE OR BREAK YOUR CHANCES FOR REPEAT BUSINESS.

Here are some suggestions for calming ruffled feathers:

Let customers vent. In fact, encourage them, but try to do it out of the public view. No matter how heated they get, remember never, never argue with a customer. Nor should you tell them "You do not have a problem." Those are fighting words!

Once they're done, politely explain your point of view. Whatever the outcome of the discussion, take action immediately to remedy the situation.

Feel like you can't stay in control? Imagine you're the one with the problem and respond in the manner in which you would like to be treated.

*But there are legal issues
you should be concerned about.*

For one, naming your site is like naming your business. You'll need to conduct a search looking for conflicts and then register your name. If you plan to use text, music or graphics on your site, find out who owns the rights to the material, and get permission to use it.

Have you hired someone to design your site? Establish upfront the ownership of the product. Are you planning to sell your product online? Then make sure your product liability insurance covers online transactions. E-commerce rules are constantly changing. Be aware of consumer privacy regulations and observe them.

If you're feeling overwhelmed right now, don't worry; you can always find an experienced consultant to help you navigate the Web.

ARE YOU PLANNING AN INTERNET SITE? WHO ISN'T?

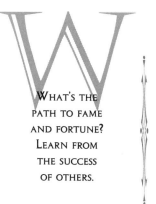

WHAT'S THE
PATH TO FAME
AND FORTUNE?
LEARN FROM
THE SUCCESS
OF OTHERS.

Here's how to start your success plan. According to Michael Jeffreys, author of Secrets of the Motivational Superstars, *you must follow three steps:*

1. First up, you need a written action plan detailing how you intend to achieve your goals. Remember, goals not written down are merely wishes. Your written goals are the road map to your success.
2. Never give up! Sure, it sounds simple, but lots of folks throw in the towel before they should. To succeed, you must be willing to do whatever it takes.
3. And finally, don't delay. You never know how much time you actually have to achieve your dreams, so you better get to it now!

SOMETIMES EVEN THE MOST ENTHUSIASTIC ENTREPRENEUR NEEDS A BOOST.

When you feel the fire in your gut start to flicker, try these tips from sales and motivational guru Barry Farber:

- *Make a commitment.* If you tell yourself you're simply not going to fail, then you'll stop trying to find excuses to quit.
- *Never stop learning.* Whether you prefer to read, listen or watch, you should always seek more information. Use books, audiotapes and CDs, videos and, of course, your computer to stretch your imagination and challenge your knowledge.
- *Accentuate the positive.* Only hang out with positive people. Negative folks tend to douse your own enthusiasm, and you can't afford to be brought down.
- *Follow the golden rule.* If you're there for other folks, chances are they'll be there for you. Building and maintaining strong relationships is key to most successful entrepreneurs.

Here are some smart tips to help you make the most of your time.

WHAT DO ALL ENTREPRENEURS HAVE IN COMMON? TOO MUCH TO DO AND NOT ENOUGH TIME TO DO IT ALL.

- At the start of the week, try to forecast any problems that might arise and come up with a tentative plan to deal with them.
- Each morning ask yourself what tasks you absolutely must accomplish that day and focus on these objectives.
- Realize you are in control of your schedule, and don't let other people get you off track.
- Plan ahead. Try to piggyback some tasks and group other activities.
- Don't forget to take a break. You'll accomplish much more if you're mentally refreshed.
- Most important, learn to say no! You have to realize sometimes you just can't do it all.

Do you network? Many entrepreneurs claim they don't have time. But networking may be vital to your success, so make the time.

To get the most out of networking, try these suggestions:

- Make sure your name is printed boldly on your nametag, which should be on your right shoulder for easy visibility.
- If you attend an event with someone you know, split up. This is not the place to talk to friends or employees.
- If you don't know anyone in the room, stand in the food or bar line. There are usually plenty of folks there to start conversations with.
- This is not the time to be shy. Smile, extend your hand and introduce yourself, but don't interrupt when others are speaking.

Remember the purpose of networking: Meet as many people as possible, and don't forget to follow up with a letter or phone call.

DID YOU KNOW THAT MOST SMALL BUSINESSES IN AMERICA ARE FAMILY-OWNED? BUT IT'S USUALLY NOT AS EASY AS IT SOUNDS TO HIRE FAMILY MEMBERS.

Before you take the plunge, ask yourself:

Does this person have the necessary experience to do the job? Would they be more valuable to the business in the long term if they first got a job elsewhere?

Once you hire a family member, make sure you clearly define their role and areas of responsibility. Make sure the person is capable of handling the job and that his or her attributes are evident to other employees.

If conflicts arise—and they will—make sure you deal with the issue at hand. Keep emotions and family history out of the discussion.

If you want to keep your business on track, it's vital that family employees are treated just like the rest of your staff. That means their salary, hours and vacation time are within company guidelines.

ARE YOUR
LEGAL COSTS
OUT OF
CONTROL?

*Here are some tips to help
lower you legal fees:*

- *First—and most obvious—
  choose the right lawyer.* You'll
  want to match his or her skills
  with your needs. And it helps if
  the lawyer has other small-business clients.
- *Determine the best fee structure
  for your business.* Will the
  lawyer charge you by the hour,
  on a contingency, or on a fixed-
  fee basis?
- *For certain legal tasks, use para-
  legals instead of attorneys.* This
  alone can save you thousands of
  dollars.
- *Don't call your attorney just to
  chat.* Usually those "small talks"
  turn into billable hours, which
  can add up.
- *Finally, don't accept—negotiate.* Ask for prompt-payment
  discounts. Even a seemingly
  small discount of 5 percent can,
  over time, be significant.

ONE OF THE HARDEST TASKS FOR MOST ENTREPRENEURS IS DELEGATION. BUT IF YOU WANT TO GROW YOUR BUSINESS, THIS WILL BE ONE OF YOUR MOST IMPORTANT LESSONS.

Here are five key steps to successful delegation:

1. *Change your attitude.* This means giving up your belief that only you can do it the right way. In other words, you need to consciously decide to give up some control.
2. *Identify tasks.* Break each job you plan to delegate into individual steps so they can be easily explained.
3. *Set limits.* Share your expectations. Explain the deadline and the quality of work that's required.
4. *Let go.* Once you explain what you want, let your workers decide how they'll tackle the task. Remember, different is not necessarily worse.
5. *Make it a habit.* Once you're comfortable delegating small jobs, try assigning larger ones. Most employees respond well to tackling greater responsibilities.

ARE YOU LIKE THE MANY ENTREPRENEURS WHO THINK YOU CAN STOP PROMOTING YOUR BUSINESS ONCE YOUR DOORS ARE OPEN?

Well, it's time to change your attitude. Smart entrepreneurs continually show their stuff.

Here are some ways you can attract attention:

- *Host an open house and invite local media and your target customers.* Let people sample your product or service.
- *Post eye-catching announcements about your business on bulletin boards in key places.* Use a tear-off slip so people can easily contact you.
- *Put magnetic signs on your car with your business's name and phone number on them.* These turn your car into a great mobile billboard.
- *Team up with compatible businesses to pass along information about your company.* Agree to do the same for them.
- *Above all, encourage your satisfied customers to spread the word,* and remember to make it worth their while.

ARE YOU A TYPICAL HOMEBASED ENTREPRENEUR, FREQUENTLY FIGHTING THE "HOME-ALONE BLUES"?

Try these ideas to fight off the isolation:

- Join your local chamber of commerce or a homebased or industry association—and attend the meetings. Networking is critical to growing businesses.
- Get out of the house. Schedule some meetings with clients over a meal. Or make sure you meet your friends or former co-workers for lunch or drinks at least once a month.
- Take a class.
- Attend conferences or trade shows.
- Give speeches about your business. You'll not only establish your expertise, but it's also a great way to market your business.
- Join forces with another homebased business owner. This is a great way to expand your client base.
- Finally, reward yourself. Take some time off, but remember to spend it outside your home.

To save money, many new business owners handle their own advertising. But it's important to ensure you're effectively spreading the message.

So before you release your ad, make sure you can answer "yes" to the following three questions:

1. *Does your ad create a sense of immediacy?* Response diminishes over time, so make sure your ad includes a call to action. Use powerful phrases like "act quickly," "call now!" or "limited-time offer."
2. *Have you hit as many "hot buttons" as possible?* People have diverse tastes. Keep the old saying "Different strokes for different folks" in mind when writing your ad.
3. *Have you evaluated other ads?* Check out all types of ads, and emulate their strengths. Remember, nothing is more wasteful than reinventing the wheel.

And this market is easier to reach than you think.

If you're like many entrepreneurs, chances are you're overlooking a lucrative market— America's 10 million Asian-Americans.

Many believe the Asian-American market is too small and too difficult to reach. But this demographic is rapidly growing and, according to Julia Huang, owner of an ad agency that targets this market, well worth pursuing. Here are some of Huang's tips:

- *Meet the market.* Go where Asian-American consumers are. Find out what they're buying and what they're interested in.
- *Check your fit.* Does your product appeal to this market? It's vital to make sure you don't inadvertently offend your targeted customers.
- *Target your pitch.* There are more than 600 Asian-language media in the United States. Most would be happy to help you create an ad with the appropriate tone in their language.

WHEN'S THE RIGHT TIME TO EXPAND YOUR BUSINESS INTO A SECOND LOCATION?

Take this four-point test and find out.

1. *Are you ready to make the effort and take the risk of owning a business you don't personally operate?* Realize it's impossible for you to be as "hands-on" in two businesses as you were in one.
2. *Is your company financially sound?* If you're not doing well in your first location, chances are your second one won't make it, either.
3. *Is your existing business running smoothly?* How much time does your current business require? Can you realistically take time and energy away from it to focus on launching a second location?
4. *Do you have the money?* You'll not only need the initial start-up capital, but you'll need operating funds as well.

Before you grow, make sure you have sufficient resources—in time, energy and cash—to meet the increased demands.

If this fear plagues you, too, here's how to overcome it:

First, you need to understand that if someone doesn't buy from you, they are not rejecting you; they're just turning down your ideas. So don't take rejection personally.

Also, when you're ready to make a sales call, remember these three key facts:

ONE OF THE MOST COMMON SALES FEARS IS THE FEAR OF COLD-CALLING.

1. *Believe in your product or service.* If you truly do, you shouldn't hesitate to interrupt someone to tell them about it. Think of your call as the chance to help someone benefit from your solution.

2. *Don't overprepare.* It's better to just take the plunge and make the call. You can't answer the potential customer's objections if you don't have the chance to hear them.

3. *Maintain a winning attitude.* Remember, if you don't expect to be successful, you won't be.

One of the most difficult things business owners have to contend with is their fear of failure.

I AM FREQUENTLY ASKED WHAT I THINK IS THE HARDEST CHALLENGE FOR ENTREPRENEURS.

But it's well past time we put this phobia behind us and face possible failure straight on.

Here in the United States, we seem particularly obsessed by the idea of winning. But no one comes out on top all the time. Take Mickey Mantle, one of the greatest baseball players of all time. Sure, Mantle hit a lot of home runs, but he struck out far more often. That didn't stop him from trying to hit those homers each time he went to bat.

So next time you're paralyzed by the fear of failing, think of the Mick and remember the words of George Bernard Shaw: "A life spent making mistakes is more useful than a life spent doing nothing."

ATTENTION, SHOP OWNERS! DO YOU HAVE AN IN-STORE SOUND SYSTEM?

No? Well, adding one could be a great opportunity to increase your sales.

Studies show that about 70 percent of all buying decisions are made by customers while they're in the store. Using a satellite music system with customized audio messages can turn empty air into an ongoing sales program.

Audio merchandising can boost impulse and add-on purchases, promote high-profit-margin goods and enhance your image. A system costs around $300 to start and runs an additional $100 a month to use. Is it worth it? Well, once they're in your store, customers are a captive audience. Who better to market to?

THERE'S NO WAY AROUND IT. WHEN YOU OWN A BUSINESS, YOU'RE IN SALES.

And one of the biggest challenges in sales is gaining a prospect's trust.

Basically, people trust people who are most like them and whom they can agree with. So you need to find out what you have in common with your customer and refer to it. This may be as simple as a shared passion for golf or foreign films. Use the similarities to bind you.

Condition your prospects by training them to agree with you. Start by asking questions they can't disagree with like "It's certainly a beautiful day, isn't it?" Once they start agreeing with you regularly, it will be a short leap to trusting you.

The three most common money personalities are achievers, money masters and entrepreneurs.

WHAT'S YOUR MONEY PERSONALITY? THERE ARE NINE DIFFERENT MONEY TYPES.

This is according to the book *Your Money Personality.*

Now I bet you think you must be the entrepreneurial type. Well, let's see. Do you seek challenges and consider money a scorecard? Entrepreneurial types are more interested in making the sale than in managing their money.

If this doesn't sound like you, maybe you're an achiever. These folks are more conservative, know how their money works for them, and trust no one else to take care of their finances.

Or are you a money master? "Value" is the key word here; money masters are bargain hunters, who always demand a cheaper price.

You can change the negative parts of your money personality, but you have to set goals and be honest with yourself.

GOT THE VOICE-MAIL BLUES? THIS TECHNOLOGY HAS SIMPLIFIED OUR LIVES, BUT IT'S ALSO CREATED A BARRIER TO REACHING PROSPECTS.

Follow these tips to make the most of voice mail:

- *First, clearly state who you are and why they should be interested in talking to you.* Then, "tease" them with the offer of some good news. This increases the odds of them returning your call.
- *Be polite, but don't sound condescending.* Use the words "please" or the phrase "I'd appreciate it if you would call me."
- *Use a fax in conjunction with your voice-mail message.* Either have your fax remind them to check their voice mail for an important message or leave a message that you'll be faxing them with items of interest.
- *When you call, leave your phone number twice, once at the beginning and again at the end of the call.* And practice saying your number slowly enough to be understood.

Whether you're seeking capital or devising a road map for success, you need a business plan.

Do you really need a business plan? You bet your business, you do.

Though you may have started your business without one, it's never too late to plot your business's fortunes.

Start by defining your business. How does your product or service fit within your industry? And what makes your company unique?

Then, define your customer. Focus in as narrowly as possible, by age, gender, ethnicity and income.

A market plan is next. Tell how you plan to get your product or service to market. Also, assess your competition and recognize their strengths and weaknesses.

When you're done writing your plan, you need to boil it down to a one- or two-page executive summary. Even though this goes at the front of your plan, it should be the last thing you write.

If you need help writing your plan, try Entrepreneur Press' *Business Plans Made Easy: It's Not as Hard as You Think.*

As an entrepreneur, you hear the word no—a lot. It's just goes with the territory.

But as the saying goes, "It's not you; it's them."

When prospects object to a sales pitch, it means they're afraid. They fear making a mistake or looking foolish. It's your job to help them overcome their fears. Start by saying "Let's explore your concerns." Then try to isolate their true objection. Here's how:

- *Offer them a choice.* For example, ask "Is it the delivery time or the financing you're concerned about?"
- *Be direct.* Find out specifically what they want to think about.
- *Be flexible.* Every sale should end up in a win-win deal, so you may need to compromise. Waive the delivery fee, offer some additional merchandise or provide marketing support.
- *Keep track.* Write down the answers to the objections you hear most often so you'll be prepared with the best response.

Tomima Edmark, inventor of the wildly successful Topsy Tail, shares her valuable insight.

ONE OF THE MOST INTIMIDATING TASKS FOR INVENTORS IS CREATING A PROTOTYPE OF THEIR IDEA.

You can find help in your local Yellow Pages. Look under model makers, industrial designers, prototype experts or product development companies.

Interview several companies. Ask to see their portfolio of prototypes. The company you choose should be familiar with your industry. And since you'll be working closely together, Edmark suggests you make sure you're compatible.

Edmark recommends that whenever possible, you should create your own prototype. After all, she says, no one knows your product as well as you do.

When the client is a nuisance, sometimes it's better to end your relationship.

ENTREPRENEURS GENERALLY WORK VERY HARD AT KEEPING EVERY CLIENT. BUT THIS IS NOT ALWAYS THE BEST WAY TO GROW YOUR BUSINESS.

How do you know when the client just isn't worth it? It may be time to say goodbye when your client:

- doesn't respect or appreciate your work;
- makes excessive demands on you or your staff;
- has unrealistic expectations of what you can do for him or her;
- isn't willing to pay a fair price for your services;
- or considers you a disposable vendor instead of a valued partner.

If you're ready to split, be sure to have a termination plan. Make the transition as smooth as possible, and maintain a professional attitude throughout the process.

*And entrepreneurs are finally
able to participate.*

One of the best ways to plan
your future is to set up a Simplified
Employee Pension Plan-Individual
Retirement Account, or a SEP-IRA
as it's called.

SEP-IRA accounts are for very
small businesses with few employees. You're eligible for opening a
SEP-IRA even if you operate a part-
time business or if you're structured as a sole proprietorship, an
S corporation or a partnership.

One of the immediate advantages of a SEP-IRA is tax savings.
Contributions are tax-deductible
for the year in which they are
made. And you can contribute
nothing or as much as 15 percent
of your net profits, or $24,000 a
year, whichever is less. To learn
more about your options, consult
a financial advisor.

W

WHAT'S THE
BIGGEST SALES
MISTAKE
ENTREPRENEURS
MAKE?

*Most entrepreneurs don't do
their homework.*

Research, says Brian Tracy, one
of the nation's best sales trainers, is
critical to successful selling. Before
you can do business with someone,
you have to understand his or her
business. Only then will you be prepared to meet their needs.

Research is not as intimidating
as it used to be. Tracy recommends
you turn first to the Internet. This
powerful tool makes it almost easy
to dig for information about companies and their industries.

If you're not "Net adept," try
the library. Or simply call the company directly. How you choose to
do it is not important; just make
sure you do it.

As the world gets smaller, smart entrepreneurs seek out global partners.

Once you find a foreign partner, here are some dos and don'ts to guide you:

Don't:
- make a commitment you can't keep.
- assume your partner understands your expectations—spell them out. And make sure you have a clear understanding of your partner's requirements.
- go without a contract. Use it to lay the groundwork for your relationship.

Do:
- find a customs broker. This person will help ensure your foreign shipments meet proper regulations.
- your homework. If you learn how business is conducted in specific countries, you can minimize potential problems.
- be prepared to pay upfront. Most international shipments are paid in advance.
- keep strengthening your relationship. If you don't get cooperation from your foreign partner, you're not going to succeed.

Why not join a link exchange for more clout?

Is your Web site underused, but you don't have the budget to drive traffic to it?

Link exchanges are essentially cyber-barter networks. Members of an exchange post fellow members' banner ads on each other's sites. Participation is free; the exchanges make money selling ads on their own sites. And you can belong to multiple programs.

The exchanges screen out adult-oriented sites from membership. Members also get a say in the types of sites where their banners appear, so you can request business-oriented or other specific sites.

Ready to join? The biggest program is linkexchange.com. If your site can use a lift, this may well be the answer.

Before a disaster hits you, make sure you're covered.

EVERY YEAR, IT SEEMS WE ENCOUNTER MORE NATURAL DISASTERS: FLOODS, HURRICANES, TORNADOES, EARTHQUAKES.

If your business is hit by a natural disaster, don't forget to claim a tax deduction for any losses. If your area qualifies for federal assistance, you can claim the deduction on the return for the year of the loss or on the prior year's tax return.

To claim the deduction, you must be able to document the loss. This includes proving you own the lost or damaged property and proving your basis in the property, which is the amount you paid for the property, plus improvements, less depreciation. Any insurance reimbursements should be deducted from the amount of the loss.

Although nothing can replace the business you worked so hard to build, at least these tax deductions offer a bit of a silver lining.

Here are some smart steps you can take to trim your expenses:

- Adjust your thermostats. Don't pay for heating or air conditioning when your building is not occupied.
- Use water-flow restrictors in sink faucets.
- Turn off all lights when they're not needed. Also, turn off equipment that's not being used.
- When replacing computers, copiers, printers, etc., buy energy-efficient equipment.
- Keep your exterior doors closed as much as possible.
- Encourage your employees to be energy-conscious. Try offering them a small reward or other incentive for energy-saving ideas.

    If these suggestions seem trivial, remember any money you save goes straight to your bottom line.

YOU CAN SAVE A LOT OF MONEY ON YOUR BOTTOM LINE JUST BY WATCHING YOUR ENERGY COSTS.

Frequently, it's a lack of capital that dooms a business before it can even get on its feet.

And according to a recent survey, the biggest potential trouble spot for entrepreneurial businesses is when they're experiencing rapid growth.

Larry Dondon, managing director of Entrepreneurs Re\$ource Group, warns entrepreneurs to avoid these common mistakes:

IS MONEY IMPORTANT TO THE SUCCESS OF YOUR BUSINESS? YOU BET IT IS!

- Failing to borrow funds
- Overlooking available financial resources
- Underestimating financial risks
- Ignoring the downside of investors
- Overestimating your borrowing potential
- Neglecting to manage lender relationships
- Preparing a loan application under pressure
- Failing to forecast cash needs

By paying attention *before* you hit the danger zone, you're more likely to avoid trouble altogether.

IQ95

These printers are now priced to fit any entrepreneur's budget.

Low-cost does not mean low-end. This new generation of printers comes loaded with features previously found only in expensive machines.

When you're ready to buy, keep these pointers in mind:

IF YOU'VE PUT OFF BUYING A LASER PRINTER BECAUSE OF COST CONCERNS, IT'S TIME TO GET OUT YOUR WALLET.

- Ask about the minimum computer requirements needed for the printer you're considering.
- Don't purchase pricey options you don't need and won't use.
- Know your RAM requirements, particularly if you print spreadsheets or graphics.
- Always get a product demonstration and check the warranties. Ask about tech support hotlines.
- And if you're in the market for more high-end equipment but cash is a problem, don't forget to check out any equipment financing options.

Yes, even in business.

SOMETIMES VIRTUE REALLY CAN BE ITS OWN REWARD.

A recent survey of American consumers indicated that a company's reputation plays a significant role in a consumer's decision to buy.

Nearly half of those surveyed said they'd be "much more likely" to buy from a socially responsible company if quality, service and price were equal. Almost 60 percent of consumers said they would be "much less likely" to buy from companies with questionable business practices. And 70 percent said they would not buy—no matter the discount—from a business that was not socially responsible.

While the survey shows that good business character pays off, the truly important message here is for businesses with less-than-sparkling reputations: Clean up your act now, before it's too late.

*Here are 10 smart ways
to keep customers:*

1. Always stress the benefits—not the features—of your product or service.
2. Exceed your customers' expectations.
3. Don't focus solely on price. Instead, point out the total value of your products or services.
4. Send customers and clients thank-you notes after making the sale.
5. Ask your customers for feedback—and follow their advice.
6. Give something extra to customers who bring you referral business.
7. Try to greet regular customers by name.
8. Keep in touch with your best customers.
9. Use special discounts to commemorate holidays and customers' birthdays.
10. Remember the golden rule, and always treat customers the way you want to be treated.

ALL ENTREPRENEURS KNOW HOW IMPORTANT IT IS TO FIND NEW CUSTOMERS. BUT IT'S EVEN MORE CRITICAL TO A BUSINESS' SUCCESS TO RETAIN THEM.

*Check out these travel tips
to help entrepreneurs
on the go keep their
travel expenses in line.*

ARE YOU
TRAVELING
MORE AND
ENJOYING IT
LESS?

- If you are departing from or traveling to an area with multiple airports, shop around for the best fares.
- When you rent a car, price all the options. Sometimes local car-rental companies offer lower rates. Does your credit card automatically provide you with increased insurance coverage? Don't pay for services you don't need.
- Always ask for the best price, especially when making hotel reservations. If there's a chance your trip might be canceled, reserve your hotel room with a credit card that guarantees your money back.
- Unless you are truly strapped for cash, don't use frequent flier miles to travel on business. Remember, business trips are tax-deductible, so it's best to charge your trip to your business credit card.

NEGOTIATING IS ONE OF THE MOST IMPORTANT SKILLS ENTREPRENEURS CAN HAVE.

Use these tips to sharpen your negotiating aptitude.

- *First, know what you want.* Establish a goal and consider what it will take for you to achieve it. Then know what the other party needs. Remember, it takes two to tango, so ask open-ended questions to gather information.
- *Listen emphatically.* What you hear is just as important as what you say.
- *The other side is not the enemy.* They are your ally and should be treated as such.
- *Be patient.* The negotiating process takes time, and, like that legendary tortoise, slow and steady wins the race.
- *Finally, be flexible.* As Mick Jagger says, "You can't always get what you want," so make sure you have a contingency plan.

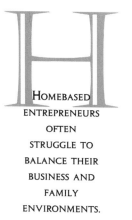

HOMEBASED ENTREPRENEURS OFTEN STRUGGLE TO BALANCE THEIR BUSINESS AND FAMILY ENVIRONMENTS.

The following ideas may help you walk that fine line.

- *Whenever possible, create a separate work space for your business.* And always use at least two different phone lines.
- *Fight the temptation to work all the time.* Establish regular work hours and keep them.
- *Set boundaries, both physical and psychological ones.* Tell your family what you expect from them and what they can expect from you.
- *Establish your own rituals.* As silly as they may appear—I knew a man who walked around the block just so he could tell himself he was on his way to work—and reversed the process in the evening—do whatever it takes to draw the line.
- *Try to give yourself a cushion when setting deadlines.* It's easier for homebased entrepreneurs to get off-schedule.

Most important, realize you cannot do it all, so don't even try!

LET'S TALK
ABOUT YOUR
SALES
MATERIALS.

*Follow these tips
to make sure your
sales materials
are up to snuff:*

- Target your sales materials to your audience. The materials should show you're a specialist with a vast knowledge of your field.
- Use testimonials in your sales letters, brochures and advertisements. These should be written by satisfied customers.
- Write your sales copy from the customer's point of view. Remember, most people are interested in helping themselves.
- Use questions in your copy. This is a great way to engage prospects' attention and pique their interest.

What if you're new to this sales thing? Don't sweat it. Instead, call attention to your innovative approach or unique product.

*If you answered "no,"
don't feel bad; enthusiasm
often wanes as new businesses
fight to get established.*

But there are ways to rekindle
your entrepreneurial fire. Try these
tips:

REMEMBER HOW
MOTIVATED YOU
WERE BEFORE
YOU STARTED
YOUR BUSINESS?
DO YOU STILL
FEEL THAT WAY?

- *Create a motivating office environment.* Surround yourself with
  positive reminders of how far
  you've come.
- *Give speeches.* Sharing your
  story with others can refresh
  your spirits, and you may even
  learn a thing or two.
- *Surround yourself with positive
  people.* Avoid those toxic people
  who drain you and poison your
  attitude.
- *Don't forget to reward yourself.*
  Create deadlines, offer yourself
  an incentive to help sweeten the
  pot and make sure you take the
  time to celebrate your victory.

Here are four smart ways to painlessly help your business grow:

1. *Develop a business plan that maps out your company's growth, and follow it.* Don't forget to update it as you grow.
2. *Buy as you grow.* Don't load up on expensive equipment until you need it. But don't be afraid to buy what you need, either.
3. *Outsource.* Almost all businesses have busy times. To get you through, try outsourcing or subcontracting some work.
4. *Know when to expand.* Compare your current level of business with past performance. Are the numbers telling you it's time to hire a permanent employee or expand to a second location? Then do it. Don't be afraid to grow.

OFTEN, NEW BUSINESSES EXPERIENCE GROWING PAINS. BUT THAT DOESN'T MEAN YOU HAVE TO SUFFER.

Do you know your competition? If you're going to survive in today's increasingly competitive business environment, you'd better.

Here are 10 questions every entrepreneur should be able to answer:

1. Who are my competitors?
2. What are their financial resources?
3. How do they market their products or services?
4. How many employees do they have?
5. Where are they located?
6. How do they treat their customers?
7. What are their pricing strategies?
8. What are their main strengths, and can I meet—or exceed—them?
9. What are their biggest weaknesses, and how can I do better?
10. How will they react to my entry into their territory?

But it's also revolutionized small-business marketing.

W̲E ALL KNOW TECHNOLOGY HAS CHANGED THE WAY WE DO BUSINESS.

There is so much software available today that almost any entrepreneur can create at least some of his or her own marketing materials. If you don't have a Web site, you should. And it's easier than ever to design your own. Once it's up, make sure you promote it, both online and offline.

You could also create newsletters, brochures and coupons to send to new and existing customers. Or how about sending colorful 6-by-9-inch postcards. Even folks who toss their so-called junk mail read these eye-catching mailers.

Any one of these ideas can generate serious profits and not blow your marketing budget.

WHAT MAKES A SUCCESSFUL SALES PRESENTATION?

Before you actually get down to business, build rapport with your prospect.

To do that, you need to do some homework. Do you have a colleague in common? Or maybe you share a passion for golf. Has the prospect's company accomplished something of note recently? Find out so the rapport is genuine.

Once you start your pitch, ask lots of questions, and make sure they require more than yes or no answers. Learn to listen. Experts say you should be listening at least 50 percent of the time.

Once you get the sale, be sure to follow up. Send a thank-you note, call to make sure they're happy, and develop a schedule for future communications.

So to be sure you cover all your bases, why not create a board of advisors?

No ENTREPRENEUR KNOWS EVERYTHING.

How you stock your advisory board depends on your business's needs and your own expertise, but it's generally a good idea to include a lawyer, an accountant, a marketing expert and a financial advisor.

When recruiting your board, make sure you ask the most successful people you can find even if you don't know them well. But be very clear about your needs and be sure to let them know you don't expect them to take an active management role or assume any liability.

It's smart to meet with your board monthly, whether as a group or individually. And remember that it's advice they're offering, not instructions. You are still the ultimate decision maker.

Sales expert and author Barry Farber shares his top sales secrets.

Farber says customers expect you to know their business—and their competition—as well as you know your own. Use annual reports, trade publications, chamber of commerce directories and the prospect's own marketing materials for research.

Answer objections with words like "feel." Farber says not to argue when a prospect says "I'm not interested." Instead, say "I understand how you feel," and then explain your company's advantages and ask for an appointment.

Once you've made a sale, ask for feedback. Farber advises new entrepreneurs to ask prospects "What do I need to do to maintain and grow our relationship?" Even if they have complaints, always give clients the chance to let you solve the problem.

There are a variety of sources start-up entrepreneurs use to fund their dreams.

READY TO START YOUR BUSINESS BUT DON'T KNOW WHERE THE MONEY IS GOING TO COME FROM?

Are you still working full time? Can you start your business part time and still collect your salary? Or can you land a part-time position while you launch your business?

Have you tried tapping family and friends? If you do, be sure to put everything in writing and treat it as a business arrangement.

If you own a home, you might consider a home equity loan. In these cases, banks either provide a lump sum or a standing line of credit.

Some entrepreneurs find credit card advances a good way to get instant cash for equipment or inventory. But be sure to use these wisely, as the interest can mount up quickly.

Buying computers and other equipment by mail can often cost lots less. For the best course of action, it's smart to check with a financial advisor.

DO YOU KNOW WHAT YOUR CUSTOMERS ARE THINKING?

You can survey them to find out, and it won't cost you a fortune.

Try telephone interviews. This is an inexpensive and fast way to get information from your customers. Ask clearly worded brief questions—people don't like to spend a lot of time on the phone answering questions.

You may learn more through a direct-mail survey. It needn't be elaborate; you can even use a postcard. But don't ask more than 15 questions.

With today's technology, you can conduct fax or e-mail interviews. The same criteria apply here—be clear and concise—and always thank customers in advance for their input.

Always remember, the most important thing is not how you ask the questions but how you apply what you learn.

*To be safe,
hire a patent attorney.*

How do you find a patent attorney you can trust? Tomima Edmark, inventor of the Topsy Tail, shares her advice.

Edmark suggests you get names from other business owners. Or ask your local or state bar association for referrals. Once you get the names of some potential attorneys, find out who some of their clients are and how long they've been practicing—look for at least three years of experience. Also make sure their area of specialization is relevant to your invention and that they file about 12 patent applications a year. Finally, advises Edmark, ask for the cost range of the last 10 applications they filed. Most important, if you're not comfortable with a lawyer, keep looking until you are.

SO MANY FOLKS HAVE GREAT IDEAS BUT DON'T KNOW HOW TO PROTECT THEM.

*Well, it might be
your own fault.*

ARE YOUR
VOICE-MAIL
MESSAGES
TOO OFTEN
IGNORED?

The most common mistake people make when leaving a message is speaking too quickly, especially when leaving their phone number. But you can easily learn to leave messages that get callbacks.

First, speak clearly, carefully enunciating each word. Give your name and phone number—twice. Be brief, but explain the reason for your call so they can be prepared when they call you back.

It's helpful to leave the date and time of your message, as well as the best time to call you back. If you are calling from a different time zone, be sure to let the person know.

Most people rely on their voice mail, so learn to make it work for you.

But if you really want to grow your business, you're going to have to attract new clientele. Here's how to find them:

First, analyze your existing customers. Your new ones will share similar traits, so the more you know about the folks you do business with now, the easier it will be to find new people.

Next, pay your existing customers a finder's fee for each new client they bring you.

Direct mail is a good way to attract new customers. Try trading mailing lists with other entrepreneurs who have similar but non-competing businesses, or contact a list broker and buy some new lists.

Finally, launch a second brand. You could go upscale, like Toyota did when they created the Lexus, or try to attract younger customers like Old Navy does for the Gap.

However you decide to expand, remember smart entrepreneurs *never* rest on their laurels.

SMART ENTREPRENEURS SHOULD ALWAYS MARKET TO THEIR EXISTING CUSTOMERS.

Then, before you start your search, make sure you do the following:

- Write a job description that clearly outlines the duties and responsibilities of the position.
- Establish a salary range and a benefits package.
- Use an "official" job application form. And once the interview process begins, make sure the information on the form matches that on the candidate's resume.
- Prepare your interview questions in advance, and ask all the candidates the same questions. Take notes during the interview so you can more accurately assess later.
- Ask open-ended questions in the interview. You want to encourage the candidate to talk, not just answer yes or no.

Finally, don't spill the beans: Find out as much as you can about them before you share details about the job.

READY TO HIRE YOUR FIRST EMPLOYEE? FIRST, BONE UP ON THE LAW SO YOU DON'T INADVERTENTLY ASK ILLEGAL QUESTIONS.

MANY ENTREPRENEURS THINK THEIR BUSINESSES ARE TOO SMALL TO WORRY ABOUT BEING SOCIALLY RESPONSIBLE.

But no company is too small to do its part.

Social responsibility starts with you, the business owner. Look around your area and see who needs a helping hand. The possibilities are endless: Retailers can donate products, restaurants usually have leftover food to give to homeless shelters, and service providers can volunteer their time and expertise.

Find out about recycling programs in your area. If you don't generate enough recyclables for your own pickup—and chances are you won't—try teaming up with other small companies to form a recycling cooperative.

Every community has its share of charitable events. Pick a few to participate in. Whether it's building housing for the homeless, litter pickup days or races for a worthy cause, try to give some money, products or time. Remember the more you give, the more you can expect to receive.

ARE YOU A CREATIVE THINKER? TOO MANY PEOPLE THINK THEY'RE NOT, BUT ALMOST ANYONE CAN LEARN TO THINK CREATIVELY.

Next time you just can't think of a new way to solve a problem, try these tips:

- *Think like a child.* Remember, childhood is the breeding ground of creative thinking.
- *Pay attention!* Great ideas are all around you. Don't hesitate to steal solutions from others and tailor them to your needs.
- *Ask everyone you know for input.* You never know who or what can spark your creativity.
- *Don't force your ideas.* If your mind is truly blank, take a break. Do something else—or do nothing at all. Getting a fresh perspective may be all you need to get you going.

Above all, have fun. Too many of us think business has to be all work, but adding an element of play can really get those creative juices flowing.

WHEN IT COMES TO PROMOTING A PRODUCT OR SERVICE, IT'S CRUCIAL TO REMEMBER TO SELL BENEFITS, NOT FEATURES.

Don't focus on what your product or service is; tell your prospects what it does.

Try to think of three good reasons customers should buy your product or service. Remember, you need to create a comfort zone so new customers will try you.

Always think about the next sale. Most sales come from word-of-mouth referrals. Make sure you create satisfactory experiences so current customers not only come back but also refer new prospects to your company.

Remember, one of the best ways to keep your customers is to prove your dedication to them.

SURE, YOU CARE ABOUT YOUR CUSTOMERS, BUT DO THEY KNOW IT?

Talk to your customers—frequently. Ask them questions, not only about what you're doing but also about what you're not.

Stay in touch. Send letters, postcards or newsletters. Let them know what's new and offer discounts and other incentives to buy.

In some businesses, entertainment is key. Find out what your best customers—or hottest prospects—like and treat them to a show, a game of golf or a ballgame.

Everyone talks about customer service, but few actually make it a manifesto. Those that do thrive. Take a hint from one of the best: Nordstrom, the department store chain. Its advice: "Use your good judgement. There are no other rules."

For most people, the very thought of public speaking is paralyzing. But it's one of the best ways to increase your presence.

Follow these tips to help conquer your fear:

First, define your goal. Who are you speaking to and why? Most important, what do you hope to accomplish?

Next, figure out what your audience wants. Is it information or inspiration, or do they expect you to solve their problems?

Practice helps banish the butterflies. Record your presentation and listen to yourself. Keep doing this until you feel—and sound—comfortable.

Finally, you want to create a lasting impression. Use colorful leave-behinds like pamphlets, fact sheets or brochures. Make sure these contain contact information and—when possible—always follow up.

*So it's imperative your
booth's design grabs them.*

IF YOU EXHIBIT
AT A TRADE
SHOW, YOU
HAVE ABOUT
FIVE SECONDS
TO CAPTURE A
PROSPECT'S
INTEREST.

Your booth should instantly tell
people who you are and what you
do. Make your graphics attractive
and bold so they command attention, even from a distance.

Develop a unique sales proposition, and use it as a headline. Does
your service or product save time,
increase productivity, do something
for less? Make sure people learn
that immediately.

Build brand identity. Coordinate
your display graphics with your
sales literature and your follow-up
mailings.

If you exhibit regularly, be sure
to keep up with the latest in booth
displays and use of technology.
Remember, you want your booth to
shine, not stand out like that
proverbial sore thumb.

YOU'VE GOT TO GET WITH THE PLAN—A SALES PRESENTATION PLAN.

Many experts recommend you go into a sales presentation with a written plan.

Writing it in advance helps you uncover possible prospect objections. If your prospect does make some objections, write them down. This shows you're really listening to what the prospect is saying.

To help the customer make a prompt decision, offer a first-time incentive. This could be an immediate discount, free shipping or bonus merchandise.

Also, offer a 100 percent satisfaction guarantee. This could make the difference for clients considering doing business with untested entrepreneurs.

It's an age-old question: Why do customers buy?

The answer is not as mysterious as you might think.

Prospects become customers because they are motivated to buy, so it's your job to appeal to their motives.

Motives are simply needs, drives and desires. And most consumers share the same basic ones, so you can figure out what motivates your clients by examining what inspires you to buy.

Most folks buy emotionally and are triggered by one or more of the following: sex appeal, social approval, status, comfort and credibility.

If your product's or service's appeal isn't apparent, it's your job to discover the prospect's motives. How? By observing and asking. Remember, human nature demands we fulfill our basic needs—food, shelter and clothing—before we more on to higher-level desires.

REMEMBER
WHEN YOU
WERE A KID
AND AN
EXASPERATED
PARENT
WARNED
"YOU'RE
PUSHING ME
TO THE LIMIT"?

While that may be bad for a kid, it's an excellent negotiation technique for entrepreneurs.

Your goal is to push the other side to their limit—but not beyond.

The first step, obviously, is to identify their immediate limit. Negotiation expert Dr. David Stiebel says there are three techniques you can use to do this:

1. *Examine their perceptions.* How much do they believe they should do for you at this point in time?
2. *Test them by pushing.* Stiebel suggests you make a proposal or take a stand and see whether they budge. If they don't, you know you've hit their limit.
3. *Check their conversational clues.* Phrases like "If I were to agree, then would you . . . ?" often indicate a change in attitude.

Remember, at this point in the negotiating process, your goal is to learn just how far your opponent is willing to go.

IS YOUR AD WORKING? IF YOU DIDN'T GET THE RESPONSE YOU WERE EXPECTING, DON'T PANIC.

First ask yourself these questions:

- *Is it a good ad in the wrong place?* Check your media plan. Did you find the medium that best targeted your audience?
- *Was the offer too weak?* How does it stack up to your competitors' ads? And don't forget to test your offer, find what works best for you, and stick with that message until it stops working for you.
- *Are there sales barriers?* Do prospects know where to reach/find you? Did you provide a toll-free phone number? Do you have a Web site where customers can find out more information and place an order? If they call, are they stuck in voice-mail hell?
- *Are you consistent?* Smart marketers build up awareness of their products or services by advertising with some degree of frequency.

IQ125

How
E-MAIL-SAVVY
ARE YOU?
USING E-MAIL
EFFECTIVELY
AND
PROFESSIONALLY
IS ESSENTIAL
TO YOUR
COMPANY'S
BOTTOM LINE.

*Try these e-mail tips
to boost your business:*

Experts recommend you include your real name, as well as your e-mail address, in your return address. This enables recipients to quickly identify you.

Next, what impression is your e-mail conveying? Check your spelling, as typos are unprofessional and indicate a lazy and careless business owner. Also remember, typing in all caps doesn't emphasize a point; rather, it means you're shouting.

As in all business communications, avoid negative wording. Positive messages get better responses than negative ones.

E-mail can be a powerful tool, so make sure yours is presented as professionally as possible.

EVERYONE KNOWS IT'S ESPECIALLY COST-EFFECTIVE TO GET EXISTING CUSTOMERS TO BUY MORE.

Try these ideas to keep 'em coming back for more:

- *Be where your customers are.* When selecting advertising and marketing opportunities, choose the ones that deliver the highest percentage of your target audience, not merely the most people.
- *Find out the negatives.* It's important to know what your customers *don't* like about your products or services, and then adjust accordingly.
- *Repeat yourself.* Smart marketers repeat the message that made the customers buy in the first place.

YOUR COMPANY'S IMAGE IS YOUR BUSINESS'S CALLING CARD.

Here's how to make the message a positive one:

- *First, create a one- or two-sentence positioning statement describing what sets you apart from your competition.* Keep it short, simple and snappy, and then communicate it in some form in all your marketing materials.
- *Don't scrimp when crafting your marketing message.* If you don't have the talent, pay for a professional to design your logo and marketing materials. You need these to represent you professionally and persuasively.
- *Use public relations to spread the word.* Don't overlook community newspapers or local radio stations when sending out press releases.

Finally, remember your goal is to build positive awareness of your business.

THERE ARE LOTS OF WAYS FOR ENTREPRENEURS TO SAVE MONEY.

Here are some you may not have thought of:

Buy recycled laser printer cartridges. Suppliers can be found in the Yellow Pages. And while we're talking about laser cartridges, use the draft mode on your printer for all internal communications and less important documents.

Get together with other entrepreneurs in your area to form buying alliances. Bulk purchases are generally much less expensive.

Buying computers and other equipment by mail can often cost lots less. But check out the mail order company's warranty and support policies before you buy.

Furniture can be found at bargain basement prices at used furniture stores, furniture rental chains and at auctions or estate sales. But make sure desk chairs are ergonomically designed, or you'll end up spending more in the long run.

Many entrepreneurs are having great success advertising on cable TV.

TTV ADVERTISING IS OUT OF THE REACH OF MOST ENTREPRENEURS— OR IS IT?

Cable ads can quickly build awareness of your business and educate consumers about what you can do for them. And with such a broad array of niche cable channels, it's easier than ever to precisely target your niche.

Now figure out who your market is and how much money you have to spend. Then call the advertising department at your local cable company. You'll want to find out about their number of subscribers and other demographic information. Make sure you completely understand the costs, not only of the TV time but of production expenses as well.

Finally, coordinating and cross-promoting all your marketing messages will give you more bang for your buck.

ARE YOU A GOOD LISTENER? IT'S IMPORTANT TO LET PEOPLE YOU'RE TALKING TO KNOW YOU REALLY HEARD THEM.

Here are some techniques you can use:

- Don't just nod your head—ask pertinent questions that allow the talker to expand or clarify what he or she is saying.
- Resist the natural temptation to make your point while the other person is still making theirs. If you're busy thinking about what you're going to say next, you're probably not really listening.
- If it's appropriate, take notes. This physically demonstrates that you're paying attention.
- If follow-up attention is required, don't forget to do so in a timely manner.

Finally, it may help to think of it this way: Listening is something you do for yourself; hearing is something you do for the other person.

MANY ENTREPRENEURS THINK THEY'RE TOO SMALL TO WORRY ABOUT FIGHTING PHONE FRAUD.

If this sounds like you, watch out because you're wrong, and if you're not careful, it will cost you.

Using default passwords programmed by the manufacturer, phone hackers can easily break into unused voice-mail boxes and rack up thousands of dollars in toll charges. Make sure all phone extensions, whether in use or not, are password-protected.

Be especially careful when using long-distance calling cards. Thieves, known as "shoulder surfers" observe callers as they punch in their account numbers in public or other unsecured areas.

The best way to protect your business from phone fraud is to analyze your bills as soon as they arrive. Look for unusual calling patterns, excessive calls to certain areas, and be particularly alert to calls to the 809 area code in the Caribbean.

I

IT'S NOT
AS HARD AS
YOU THINK TO
UNCOVER YOUR
COMPETITORS'
SECRETS.

*But first you need to know
who your competitors are.*

Local rivals can probably be
found in the Yellow Pages, online or
through your chamber of commerce. Finding national competition
takes a broader approach. Start
with a trip to the library. Industry
associations, trade publications and
an Internet search can help turn up
some names.

The best way to get the scoop is
at the source. Try to question their
customers. Go to their stores, buy
their products or use their services,
and evaluate their policies. Then
determine how you can beat them.

*But how do you use
your company's Web site
most effectively?*

First, know why you're building a site. Is your goal to advertise, sell, build a prospect list, or some combination of the above and hundreds of other possibilities? You don't need to limit yourself, but you should define what you expect your site to do for you.

Realize that Web marketing is still so new, you should set nothing in stone. Be experimental and don't overplan—you'll lose valuable time. Keep some money in your budget for after you launch your site because it's hard to know what works until after you're actually online.

The Net is crowded, so make sure you register with as many search engines as possible. And promote, promote, promote. This is one area where "if you build it, they will come" definitely does *not* apply.

OK, BY NOW, WE ALL KNOW THE WEB WORKS FOR BOOSTING BUSINESS.

LET'S GET DIRECT—WITH DIRECT MARKETING. SOMETIMES THE BEST WAY TO INCREASE YOUR SALES IS TO GO STRAIGHT TO THE SOURCE.

Here are some suggestions on how to make direct marketing work for you:

Why not send old customers who you haven't heard from in the past six months a discount coupon? Bargains are usually great motivators.

If you want to poll your customers, it's traditional to give a monetary incentive. Sending the unexpected usually increases response—try a two-dollar bill for a change.

Acknowledge your customers' birthdays or other special occasions with a special offer. It may sound sentimental, but customers love the attention, and that translates into increased sales.

Direct marketing guru Jerry Fisher recommends you send a "lumpy" mailer. Few, says Fisher, can resist opening an envelope with a lump or small box in it.

Why bother with direct marketing? Because it is especially designed to get people to stop ogling and start ordering. Try it, and you'll see.

But it's vital to do so.
Here are some smart ideas:

Busy HOMEBASED ENTREPRENEURS ON THE GO KNOW IT'S OFTEN HARD TO STAY IN TOUCH WITH THE OFFICE WHILE ON THE ROAD.

- Before you leave, let your most important clients know you're leaving—and when you're coming back.
- Leave a message on your answering machine stating how long you'll be gone, when you'll be back, and how often you'll be checking your messages. If possible, try to return important calls the same day you receive them.
- Don't forget to take advantage of e-mail. It's an efficient and relatively inexpensive way to keep in touch.
- Finally, check ahead with your hotel to find out what kinds of business services it offers. Make sure you give your important clients all your contact numbers. This not only keeps your customers happy, but it makes your life less hectic when you return.

But there are some smart ways to make your site globally friendly:

A WEB SITE IS IMPORTANT TO BUILDING AN INTERNATIONAL BUSINESS. BUT REMEMBER, NOT ALL NATIONS USE THE SAME EQUIPMENT OR WEB STANDARDS.

- Keep images to a minimum. Not only can they slow the down-loading process, but, in many cases, images developed for the American marketplace may not be relevant or they're misunderstood by global users.
- Make sure your site is easy to navigate. Don't try to dazzle the user with cleverness. Provide clear instructions and text guidelines.
- Use international formats for dates, times and currencies. For instance, instead of 3:30 p.m., say 15:30.
- Develop an e-mail response form that includes automated options, such as radio buttons. This minimizes the amount of translation needed.
- Make it easy for customers to request information via e-mail.

Try these tips:

The best time to bill customers is as soon as it's practically possible. Service providers can bill clients the day the service is completed—or sooner if you incur substantial expenses along the way. If you send products to customers, include the invoice with the shipment.

Make sure your invoice is professionally designed, with the word "invoice" clearly printed across the top. Your company's name, address and phone number should also be prominent.

Send the invoice to the person responsible for remitting payment. Your invoice should describe the product or service provided, specify the exact charges, state the total amount due, and identify the person who placed the order.

To speed payment, state "payment due upon receipt" on your form. A smart way to really speed the process is to offer a discount if the bill is paid within 10 days.

MANY START-UP ENTREPRENEURS SUFFER FROM CASH FLOW PROBLEMS. SMART HANDLING OF YOUR INVOICES CAN HELP EASE THIS SITUATION.

But that only gets your foot in the door. At some point, you've got to prove you're as good as—or better than—everyone else.

Now that you're a supplier, you may be dealing with different people than you did before. In fact, some of your former co-workers may even view you as a threat to their job security or be envious of your new entrepreneurial status.

Here are some tips to make the transition an easy one:

- Make sure the people you're now dealing with are comfortable with any relationships you may still have with former co-workers.
- Your ex-colleagues can make strong allies. Enlist their aid whenever possible.
- Finally, don't expect to be told company secrets or to coast through your projects. Remember, you don't work there anymore.

SMART ENTREPRENEURS OFTEN START THEIR BUSINESSES WITH FORMER EMPLOYERS AS CLIENTS.

ONE OF MY PET PEEVES IS THE MANY INANE ZONING REGULATIONS THROUGHOUT THE COUNTRY THAT LIMIT THE OPERATION OF HOMEBASED BUSINESSES.

If it's illegal to operate a homebased business in your area, don't just sit there.

Here are some steps you can take to change local zoning laws:

First, establish a committee of homebased business owners and other interested parties who are willing to take a stand. Get ready for a barrage of criticism—and the possibility your business could be shut down.

Next, find out about the zoning regulations in neighboring communities, especially those that are like your town or city. If operating home businesses is legal there, it could help you build your case.

Then contact your local zoning office to see if it has received complaints about illegally operated home businesses. Chances are they haven't, which can bolster your argument that most homebased entrepreneurs are quiet and don't cause problems.

See the next tip for more information on legalizing homebased businesses.

First, do your research.

Gather the facts and statistics to show how much homebased entrepreneurs pay in business licenses and taxes.

Once you've assembled your research arsenal, use the information to build a coalition to support a new ordinance. Draft other home business owners, government officials, representatives from big businesses that use the services of homebased entrepreneurs, homeowner's associations, and anyone else with a vested interest in your cause.

Finally, remember your goal is first to educate, then to mobilize community support. Most important—stand up and be counted! Homebased businesses contribute a lot to their communities and local economies. It's well past time they were able to operate in the open.

TO MAKE HOMEBASED BUSINESSES LEGAL IN YOUR AREA, YOU NEED TO SHOW HOW THEY CONTRIBUTE TO THE COMMUNITY'S ECONOMY.

ONCE A YEAR, THINK SPRING— SPRING CLEANING, THAT IS, AND TIME TO CLEAN YOUR COMPUTER.

Here are some smart pointers:

- Dust the outside of your CPU case and keyboard. Use an anti-static spray on your monitor to keep it easy to read.
- Take the CPU case off and blow compressed air into any parts that may have gotten dusty.
- Turn your keyboard upside down over a trashcan and gently shake it to loosen any grit inside.
- Don't forget your mouse. Remove the cover that holds the mouse's ball in place. Using that handy can of compressed air— or your finger—remove any grime on the mouse ball and inside the compartment. Make sure you pay close attention to the rollers.
- Lastly, don't forget what's "in" your computer as well. Don't go too crazy, but get rid of any unwanted files. Do *not* delete any files ending with .dat, .dll, .exe, .ini, or .sys. You can always make archive copies of files you don't want cluttering up your hard drive.

Even using the most sophisticated presentation technology won't help you make the sale if you haven't polished your presentation skills.

Here are six smart ways to come across like a pro:

1. *Stay loose.* If you feel tight, you'll likely come across as cold or unsure of yourself.
2. *Connect with your audience.* Make sure you talk to them in terms they understand. Watch them, and address their concerns on the spot.
3. *Use body language to project confidence.* Stand or sit solidly, don't sway or waver, but don't be stiff, either.
4. *Speak up.* Make sure your tone conveys conviction and authority. And don't forget to project so listeners can clearly hear you.
5. *Don't hide your passion.* Your enthusiasm and energy will help you make your case. And clients want to know you will feel strongly on their behalf.
6. *Most important, relax—and don't forget to smile.* Remember, you are communicating with real people who are seeking to make a connection with you. In other words, be yourself.

It's your handshake.

Experts say how you shake hands says a lot about who you are and how you feel about yourself.

To send a positive message, extend your hand with the thumb up and open. Wrap your fingers around the other person's hand and shake once or twice from the elbow, not the shoulder. This results in a firm handshake that is neither too weak nor too strong.

At networking events, make sure you keep your right hand free so you'll always be ready to shake hands. That means carrying your briefcase or purse in your left hand. At cocktail parties, hold your glass in your left hand, so your right one doesn't get cold or wet.

In our culture, handshakes mean a lot. Make sure you do it every time you're introduced to someone and at the beginning and end of every meeting.

HERE'S SOMETHING MOST ENTREPRENEURS DON'T EVEN THINK ABOUT, BUT IT CAN MAKE A BIG DIFFERENCE IN HOW YOU'RE PERCEIVED.

And here are some reasons why:

Perhaps the most important reason to put a business plan into writing is that the very process forces you to think through what you're doing and where your business is headed.

But that's not the only reason smart entrepreneurs write business plans. Here are some others:

If you plan to borrow money, you'll need to show a written plan. Whether you're approaching a bank, outside investors, the Small Business Administration, or others for cash, you'll be required to show a plan that demonstrates your ability and knowledge about your industry.

A business plan serves as both a historical document and a guide to the future. It lets you see what worked—and what didn't.

Don't put off writing your plan. There are plenty of books and software to help you. Or ask your financial advisor for assistance.

AS I'VE SAID BEFORE, THERE'S NO WAY AROUND IT— YOU NEED A BUSINESS PLAN.

HOMEBASED ENTREPRENEURS OFTEN FIND IT DIFFICULT TO MAINTAIN THE BOUNDARIES BETWEEN WORK AND BUSINESS.

Here are some smart ways to maintain control:

- *Set business hours—and keep them.* Let your clients know when you're open for business and that when it's 5 or 6 o'clock, the office is closed.
- *Get a dedicated business phone line that routes unanswered calls into voice mail or an answering machine.* After hours, even if you're still working, let the equipment take the call.
- *Use a pager, especially if you travel or have a number of clients outside your local area.* Tell your clients to page you, and then you control when to return the call.
- *Finally, encourage your clients to use faxes or e-mail whenever possible.* That means always keep your fax machine on, and check your e-mail regularly.

WHAT'S IN A NAME? PLENTY. SO YOU'D BETTER MAKE SURE YOUR COMPANY'S NAME CONVEYS THE PROPER MESSAGE.

Here are some things to think about:

- What does your company's name communicate? Your business's name should reinforce key elements of your business. Are you upscale, convenient or a bargain? Your name should tell the tale.

- Is your name too cute or obscure to mean anything to strangers? Avoid meaningless initials or cute names that only you understand. And if you're planning to expand, don't limit your business by using a geographic name.

- Is your name suggestive, which is more abstract, or is it descriptive, telling something about your business, such as what it does or where it is?

- How about the competition? What approach do they take? Make sure your name distinguishes you from the pack.

ALL ENTREPRENEURS WATCH THEIR PENNIES. BUT WHEN IT COMES TO CERTAIN LEGAL MATTERS, YOU DON'T WANT TO GO IT ALONE.

Often it's smart to consult with an attorney. Here are a few examples:

- *Written agreements:* Do your lease agreements and purchase contracts indicate the specific duties and expectations of each party?
- *Licensing and ordinances:* Do you need to be licensed or bonded? Is liability insurance required?
- *Business structure:* Should you incorporate or stay a sole proprietorship?
- *Employer-employee relations:* Are you familiar with the laws that govern hiring employees? Do you need an employee handbook?
- *Partnerships:* If you don't have a partnership agreement in place, you could lose your business.

Don't be penny-wise and pound-foolish when it comes to your business's future. A little legal advice can go a long way.

Take a look at your client list and see if there's anyone you'd be better off without.

BELIEVE IT OR NOT, SOMETIMES IT'S SMART TO TURN DOWN BUSINESS. START-UP ENTREPRENEURS IN PARTICULAR OFTEN SAY YES TO EVERY CLIENT THAT COMES ALONG.

For instance, do you have clients who are never satisfied with your products or services, no matter how hard you try? Or do some of your clients think the rules don't apply to them? Are they consistently late paying bills? Do they demand more than their fair share of attention or expect 'round-the-clock care? Maybe some clients are simply taking up too much of your time to be worthwhile.

If any of this sounds familiar to you, it might be time to say good-bye. Of course, you should never deliberately offend a client. Break the relationship off gently, but never leave a client in the lurch. Remember, what comes around goes around.

EVEN THE MOST SUCCESSFUL BUSINESSES CAN ENCOUNTER A CASH FLOW CRISIS. SINCE A CASH CRUNCH COULD CRIPPLE YOUR BUSINESS, IT'S SMART TO BE PREPARED.

Here's how:

- *Establish a rainy-day fund.* Set cash aside in an interest-bearing account you can draw on in an emergency.
- *Review your current cash-management techniques.* Don't pay bills until you have to, but take advantage of early-payment discounts. Ask your banker about special programs to help you better manage your money.
- *Control your overhead.* Keep your fixed costs low and your variable expenses tied to revenue, so if your income drops, so will your expenditures.
- *Establish and maintain good credit.* If you have a good track record, creditors may be more willing to work with you in times of crisis.
- *Finally, find a financial advisor you trust.* Chances are they'll know what to do even when you don't.

Once you find a potential leasing company, ask the salesperson—and yourself—these questions:

SOMETIMES IT IS SMARTER TO LEASE RATHER THAN BUY EQUIPMENT. HOW DO YOU KNOW?

- What equipment do I need, and how long will I need it?
- How much can I afford to pay monthly?
- Are there tax advantages or dis-advantages?
- Can I show my financial advisor a sample copy of the lease?
- How is this lease terminated? Are there buyout options? Are they negotiable?
- Can I upgrade at no cost? Are there time limits?
- How flexible is the payment schedule?
- Do you service and/or repair the equipment?

Once you get your answers, don't jump at the first lease offered. Shop around, do your homework, and consult with your financial advisor.

DO YOU KNOW WHAT YOUR COMPETITORS ARE UP TO? YOU SHOULD— OR YOU COULD END UP LOSING BUSINESS TO THEM.

Here are some smart ways to check out the competition:

- *Request information.* Call for a price list, a brochure or other marketing information. Evaluate how you were treated on the phone, how the request was processed, and how long it took to get answers.
- *Order something.* Have a friend order something from your competition and from your company. Compare and contrast the two experiences.
- *Pay a visit.* Note the differences between your business and theirs.
- *Compare everything.* Think price, packaging, marketing, selection, quality, delivery and attitude.

When the comparisons are over, be ready to react. Implement any necessary changes as soon as possible.

YOU'RE ABOUT TO MAKE A BIG PRESENTATION. YOU'RE READY, BUT IS YOUR EQUIPMENT?

Here's how to make sure everything comes together:

- *Don't overdo it.* If you use every flying bullet and unique effect that comes with your presentation software, you'll drive your audience crazy. For maximum impact, keep these features to a minimum. Remember, you don't want to distract your viewers.
- *Think big.* Display text in at least 24-point type. Use serif fonts for large titles only; use sans serif in the main body of your presentation.
- *Be organized.* Every presentation needs some kind of structure. One basic yet effective structure includes an introduction or agenda, key points, a closing and some recommendations.
- *Spell it out.* Avoid just mentioning statistics—tell your audience exactly what they mean.

Sometimes it's best to say it in words.

Here are four tips to writing winning sales letters:

1. *Pretend you're the customer.* Imagine yourself as the reader of your letter, and write what the customer wants to know, not what you want to say.
2. *Organize your letter.* Good sales letters need an introduction, a body and a conclusion. First, tell why you're sending the letter. Then make your sales pitch in the body of the letter, and bring all your points together at the end.
3. *Make it easy to read.* Write conversationally, using short sentences and paragraphs. And edit and re-edit your letter. Typos and grammatical errors destroy your credibility.
4. *Most important, ask your readers to take action.* State what you want them to do, whether it's to call, visit or send for more information.

*Here's how to make sure
your employees know
exactly what to do:*

EVEN IF YOU
HAVE ONLY ONE
EMPLOYEE, IT'S
IMPERATIVE HE
OR SHE BE
PROPERLY
TRAINED,
ESPECIALLY
WHEN IT COMES
TO SERVING
YOUR
CUSTOMERS.

First, tell your staff why you want to train them and then promptly start a program. Schedule the sessions during breakfast or lunch and provide the meal. Rent or buy audio and video training programs. Some may even be available at your local library.

Reward positive performance. Verbal feedback is always appreciated. Consider rewarding superior behavior in a more tangible way.

This sounds silly, but make sure everyone—including you—smiles when they're on the phone. Customers can hear the smile in your voice, and it can have a big impact. Finally, remember training sessions don't have to be long. Fifteen to 20 minutes a day can be worth thousands of dollars in improved performance.

WANT TO BUILD A GREAT COMPANY? YOU CAN.

Try these tips from James Collins and Jerry Porras, authors of Built to Last: Successful Habits of Visionary Companies:

- *Be a clock builder, not a time teller.* Time tellers are charismatic leaders with great ideas, but clock builders build a "clock" that runs even in their absence. Most entrepreneurs are time tellers—to succeed, you must make the switch.
- *Build your company on core values.* All great companies, large and small, are built on a rock-solid set of core values. Most have a clear sense of purpose beyond just making money.
- *Be willing to change everything—except your core values.* Small companies stay small when they're fixated on their first products or strategies. Small businesses become big businesses when they're willing to change and progress, yet remain true to their basic value system.

So here's how to figure it out for yourself:

How are you doing? As a start-up entrepreneur, it's often hard to know. But everyone needs feedback.

What tasks do you need to do to accomplish your goals? Write them on a calendar. This lets you manage your daily work flow and gives you a view of the big picture at the same time.

Time is your most valuable asset, so keep track of it. Software programs make it easy to record your billable and nonbillable work.

Ask a spouse, friend or relative to hold you accountable for your goals. This way you can't shrug them off as something you don't really have to do.

Finally, acknowledge your achievements. Reward yourself with great meal, a good book or even a day off. It's important to pat yourself on the back.

Following are six ways to do that:

WHAT'S THE KEY TO SMALL-BUSINESS SUCCESS? WELL, ONE IMPORTANT COMPONENT IS, OBVIOUSLY, KEEPING YOUR CUSTOMERS SATISFIED.

1. *Find out what your customers want.* Don't guess—ask them through surveys, focus groups, any way you can.
2. *Dazzle them with service so remarkable they'll tell their friends and colleagues.* Nothing works like word-of-mouth marketing.
3. *Be responsive.* Don't make your customers wait for service, not on the phone or in your store. Take care of their needs immediately.
4. *Never deceive your customers.* Eventually, they'll find out, and they'll never come back to you.
5. *Reward your clients.* Offer frequent-buyer programs, volume discounts or other incentives that show you appreciate their business.
6. *If it's wrong, make it right.* Even if the mistake is not your fault, fix it!

EVEN IN THIS ERA OF INSTANT COMMUNICATIONS ENTREPRENEURS CAN'T AVOID USING THE MAIL. AND DON'T THINK YOUR BUSINESS IS TOO SMALL TO GET MAILING DISCOUNTS.

Try these smart postal pointers:

- *Clean up.* The post office can clean your mailing list—for free. They'll correct addresses, note incomplete addresses and add ZIP-plus-4 codes so you'll be eligible for bar-code discounts.
- *Bulk up.* If you mail in bulk, consider purchasing a standard-mail permit. Although the permit costs around $85 a year, you'll pay substanially less than first-class rates.
- *Shop around.* Delivery rates vary among carriers. Compare rates and ask about small-business discounts.
- *Mail early.* In many cases, this results in one- to two-day delivery—all for the price of a first-class stamp!

ENTREPRENEURS
ON THE GO
CAN TRAVEL
FOR LESS.
THE KEY IS TO
PLAN AHEAD
AND SHOP
AROUND.

*Here are some
travel-smart suggestions:*

Consider purchasing prepaid phone cards. These typically offer a flat rate of less than 20 cents per minute, significantly less than what it costs to dial direct during weekday business hours. Plus, you avoid paying the frequently higher rates charged from phone booths and hotels.

Hotel rooms don't have to cost you a fortune. You can often save 10 percent to 40 percent by booking your rooms through a consolidator. Or when booking your room, ask about any available discounts for business travelers or members of a group you may belong to.

Try to take advantage of frequent flier miles. You can book your flights on one airline, or use a credit card that accumulates miles from several airlines.

Whatever your travel plans, remember it pays to shop around, and always ask for the best deal.

But even the smallest businesses can use community outreach as a low-cost, high-impact marketing tool.

The benefits of civic marketing are plentiful: It raises community awareness of your business, builds customer and employee loyalty, helps you stand out from your competitors, and positions you as a community leader.

Select your causes carefully. Look for ones truly meaningful to your community, your industry or your target market.

Depending on your situation, you can donate money, time or resources. Some business owners encourage their employees to volunteer at the charity or cause of their choice. Others may establish scholarships for high school or college students.

Whatever your involvement, don't forget to use public relations campaigns, promotional signs or in-store displays to let the community know what you're up to.

"CIVIC MARKETING"— THE KIND PRACTICED BY FOLKS LIKE BEN & JERRY— IS ONE OF THE NEWEST BUSINESS BUZZWORDS.

Turn your card over, and what do you see?

If you're like most entrepreneurs, your answer is "nothing." But smart business owners are using the backs of their cards as a key part of their marketing arsenal.

George Allen, a real estate entrepreneur in Indiana, includes a loan amortization chart or a return-on-investment formula on the backs of his cards.

Allen, who's writing a book about the power of business cards, believes almost any entrepreneur can take advantage of this idea.

What you print on your card will depend on your industry or business. Or try these suggestions: a calendar, a useful chart or graph, a map of your location, a photo of an unusual product, a memorable or inspirational quote, a coupon, or a glossary of industry terms.

Remember, the idea is to use your card to make your business memorable and your business card a keeper.

ARE YOU OVERLOOKING THE MARKETING POTENTIAL OF YOUR BUSINESS CARD? YOU MAY QUICKLY ANSWER "OF COURSE NOT," BUT I BET YOU ARE.

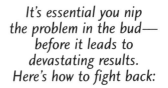

It's essential you nip the problem in the bud— before it leads to devastating results. Here's how to fight back:

A AT SOME POINT, YOUR BUSINESS MAY FALL VICTIM, WARRANTED OR NOT, TO NEGATIVE WORD-OF-MOUTH.

The best way to counter negativity is to create positive word-of-mouth. Try to get to the source of the problem and specifically answer the charges.

Negative comments are often spread by discontented customers. Compile your customer complaints, and see if there's a pattern. Do you have a problem with a particular product or service? Or could a disgruntled employee be the cause? The best way to find out is to ask customers what they think about your business.

Finally, plan ahead. Have emergency plans in place in case there is a problem. And if you encourage an open relationship with your customers, you'll likely be able to head off problems before they happen.

IQ163

But don't jump blindly into a partnership before you do your homework.

TEAMING UP WITH BIGGER BUSINESSES IS A SMART WAY ENTREPRENEURS CAN GROW THEIR COMPANIES.

First, check references. That's plural—more than one. If the company won't provide you with a list, it's likely it is hiding something.

Try to find some references on your own. Ask your industry colleagues, community leaders or whomever you think is relevant what they've heard about your potential partner.

Visit the other business's location. You can learn a lot just by looking around. Pay particular attention to the company's organization, safety record, employee morale and overall office environment.

Finally, no matter how appealing it sounds, don't pay for products, services or representation in advance. And in the beginning, don't sign long-term contracts, and always include an escape clause.

Well, join the crowd.

Do you believe in selling the sizzle instead of the steak?

But guerrilla marketing guru Jay Conrad Levinson believes that's just one of several marketing myths entrepreneurs should ignore. In reality, Levinson says, smart entrepreneurs don't sell the sizzle—or the steak—they sell solutions to problems.

Here are three other marketing myths Levinson says we'd all be better off ignoring:

Myth No. 1: People don't like to read, so only use short copy in your ads. "Bunk!" says Levinson. People read whatever interests them, no matter how short—or long—it is.

Myth No. 2: Small businesses can't afford to advertise on television. Maybe not on the networks, but you should check the rates for cable and satellite-delivered programming.

Myth No. 3: Any publicity is good publicity. "No," says Levinson. "Bad publicity is bad for business."

BUILDING SUCCESSFUL MAIL ORDER ENTERPRISES IS ONE WAY SMALL ENTREPRENEURS CAN BECOME BIG-BUSINESS OWNERS.

Follow these hints to help you become a mail order wizard:

- Study the competition to help you learn what's hot and what to avoid.
- Join a trade association, and pay attention to industry experts. Many predict annual trends based on extensive—and expensive—research.
- Don't try to be a one-product wonder; it rarely works. Develop piggyback products to broaden your appeal.
- Consider selling products outside your industry that would interest your customers. For example, florists could sell floral books, stationery or even jewelry in addition to flowers.
- Watch your costs. Catalog expenses are rising. Make sure postage and handling costs are covered. And don't overlook the Internet as an additional or alternative way to sell products.

According to industry experts, paperwork can be a homebased business owner's biggest burden.

IS YOUR HOMEBASED OFFICE A MESS? DON'T FEEL BAD IF YOUR ANSWER IS YES.

If you're not organized, you're wasting time—and for all entrepreneurs, time is money. Here are some smart ways to unclutter your workplace:

First, sort all your paperwork by category, and put it into clearly marked file boxes. Don't keep what you don't need.

Organize your work space. How many file cabinets do you really need? What can be boxed and stored elsewhere? Items you use every day should be within easy reach; everything else should be put away.

At the end of your workday, always put things back where they belong. Remember, staying organized is like any good habit—the more you practice it, the easier it becomes.

Nervous? Don't be. Remember, it's your business and you're in control of the interview.

You should have a number of questions to ask prospective employees. But here are four basic questions you should ask in every job interview:

GETTING READY TO HIRE YOUR FIRST EMPLOYEE? AFTER SORTING THROUGH COUNTLESS RESUMES, IT'S TIME TO TACKLE THE JOB INTERVIEW.

1. What's the greatest asset you'll bring to this company? This question is a great icebreaker and sets the interviewee at ease.
2. What's your greatest weakness? Asking this still surprises many and the answer is key to how the candidate thinks on his or her feet.
3. What was your favorite and least favorite job? Look here for the candidate's ability to objectively evaluate a situation rather than subjectively react to it.
4. And the ever-popular "Where do you see yourself in five years?" The right answer here should reflect a wish list of increased responsibilities.

If not, read on.

Keep in mind you can only ask job candidates questions that directly bear on their ability to perform the job. Do not ask their age, date of birth, race, creed, color, religion or national origin. Also avoid questions about any disabilities they may have, the date and type of military discharge, or marital status.

Women should not be asked about their maiden names, if they have children, how many they have, or who will watch them while they're working.

Don't ask candidates if they've ever been treated for drug addiction, alcoholism or if they've ever sought psychological counseling. And you cannot ask if they've ever been arrested.

The hiring process is an arduous one. Take your time, be prepared, and make sure you cover all your legal bases.

OK, YOU KNOW WHAT THE BEST QUESTIONS ARE TO ASK A JOB CANDIDATE IN AN INTERVIEW, BUT DO YOU KNOW WHAT QUESTIONS YOU LEGALLY CANNOT ASK?

One of the keys to success is knowing how to close the sale.

Here's how you can become a better closer.

Don't try to close prematurely. First, make sure you've satisfied the prospect's needs and concerns, and that he or she believes you can solve the problem at hand.

Then ask for the final decision. This sounds obvious, but it's often overlooked by the inexperienced, who instead wait for the *prospect* to seal the deal.

If you're uncomfortable with the term "closing," think of it as helping someone make a decision. Don't take a heavy-handed approach. Instead, in a fun, nonthreatening way, ask "So how many do you want?" or "We have it in a rainbow of colors. Do you want them all?"

Still worried? Remember, your ultimate goal is to get the business, so don't be afraid to ask for it.

MOST NEW ENTREPRENEURS, NO MATTER THEIR BUSINESS, HAVE TO SELL SOMETHING, WHETHER IT'S A PRODUCT, SERVICE, OR EVEN THEMSELVES.

The key to RADAR is asking questions, and if done right, it will tell you if the prospect is worth spending time with. Here's how RADAR works:

1. *Rapport:* Is the prospect answering your questions honestly?
2. *Acknowledged interest:* Does the prospect see that he has a problem, and is he interested in solving it?
3. *Decision:* Find out who the decision makers are.
4. *Acknowledged funds:* How much energy, time and money is the prospect willing to invest?
5. *Risk coefficient:* Has the prospect ever purchased a similar product or service? Yes means the prospect has a positive risk coefficient, and you have a good chance of landing the account. If not, make sure this person is worth the extra time you're going to have to invest.

A two-minute RADAR conversation with the prospect should give you your answer.

DON'T KNOW HOW MUCH TIME TO DEVOTE TO NEW PROSPECTS? TRY THE **RADAR** SYSTEM, DEVELOPED BY SALES TRAINER JEFFREY HANSLER.

MANY EXPERTS SAY TIME IS THE MOST IMPORTANT COMMODITY FOR NEW HOMEBASED ENTREPRENEURS.

But time is a limited resource, so use yours wisely. Here's how:

- *Organize your work space to streamline your operation.* That means make it as clutter-free as possible, and keep frequently used items in front of you.
- *Use lists to keep track of tasks.* Ask yourself "What is the most important thing to do?" and establish a priority list.
- *Do your most vital tasks at your peak time of the day.* Everyone has times when his or her energy and focus are highest. Figure out when yours are, and give yourself an uninterrupted two hours to accomplish your most important tasks.
- *Make every minute count.* A cordless phone is a must here— you can talk and do other things at the same time. Double up whenever possible.

LOOKING TO EXPAND OVERSEAS? MANY BUSINESSES THAT DO SO FAIL, SO BE SURE TO PREPARE FOR YOUR MEETING WITH YOUR POTENTIAL PARTNERS.

To avoid making costly mistakes in your overseas meeting, follow these tips:

- *Build a relationship before you get down to business.* This entails making small talk before business talk.
- *Don't impose time limits.* Keep the meeting as open as possible; this will add strength to your negotiating position.
- *Do your homework.* Learn at least a bit about the country you're in; this shows respect for your potential partner's culture.
- *Bring your own interpreter.* Their interpreter will have their interests at heart.
- *Understand everyone's body language.* Americans think body language is universal—it's not!

Finally, despite our current fascination with casual, dress with authority and respect.

The Labor Department has set five criteria for distinguishing interns from employees.

1. Training must consist of experiences similar to those offered in a vocational school.
2. Interns cannot replace regular employees, and they must work under close observation and supervision.
3. At the end of the internship, the intern is not necessarily entitled to a job. If they are, the internship looks like a training program, and the interns would be entitled to a fair wage.
4. Both you and the intern must acknowledge that he or she is not entitled to wages.
5. The training must be primarily for the intern's benefit. That means no coffee-making or errand-running. Interns are not go-fers or secretaries—they are there to learn.

And remember, interns have the same legal rights as employees. It's smart to cover them under a workers' compensation package.

THINKING OF HIRING A FREE INTERN? BE CAREFUL. YOUR INTERNS MAY LOOK LIKE EMPLOYEES, WHICH CAN GET YOU INTO A LOT OF TROUBLE.

Here's how:

First, use a standard credit application form for every customer. The application should list the company's legal name, the name it operates under and the principal's names. It also should provide complete contact information, including who has the authority to make purchases and who to call about invoices; both physical and mailing addresses; phone, fax and e-mail numbers; and any special instructions required.

Next, either on the application or on another form, clearly state your terms and the consequences for failing to meet them. This could include late fees, legal fees if action becomes necessary, and where any lawsuit would be filed.

Of course, make sure the customer signs the document. And don't forget the obvious—ask for and check credit references.

OK, YOU'VE MADE THE SALE. BUT ARE YOU GOING TO GET PAID? BEFORE YOU EXTEND CREDIT, MAKE SURE YOU ESTABLISH CREDIT POLICIES.

TIMING IS
EVERYTHING,
RIGHT? YES,
ESPECIALLY
WHEN IT COMES
TO MARKETING.

*To get the most for your
marketing dollar, make sure you
properly time your efforts.*

- Try to ensure that your direct-
  mail package arrives Tuesday,
  Wednesday or Thursday.
- When relevant, tie your message
  to what's going on in the world.
- Don't launch your marketing too
  soon. Make sure you have
  worked all the bugs out, that
  your salespeople know all the
  facts, and that you can deliver
  on what you promise.
- If you're in retail, wait a month
  before you have your grand
  opening celebration. This way,
  you will be more practiced.
- Don't waste time telemarketing
  when nobody's there. Find out
  the best time to call.
- Never rush through the creation
  of your marketing materials. The
  key words to keep in mind here?
  Economy and quality. Remember,
  when it comes to marketing,
  speed can kill.

USP stands for unique selling proposition, and it's what sets you apart from your competitors. Here's how to establish your USP:

ALL ENTREPRENEURS, ESPECIALLY NEW ONES, NEED A USP. WHAT'S YOURS? OK, FIRST I'LL EXPLAIN.

First, determine what benefits customers will receive when they purchase your product or service. This can be based on how your business operates, the quality of your work or any other element that makes you stand out.

Then, make sure your competition doesn't offer the same proposition. You can't be as good as they are; you have to be better. This isn't as hard as it sounds. Your competitors might have the same qualities, but perhaps they don't capitalize on them. If you define the benefit and educate the customer, you've gained the advantage.

Don't take your USP lightly. It must be strong enough to continually attract new customers. If handled correctly, your USP will come to define you and your business.

IS IT POSSIBLE
TO GET MORE
AND SPEND LESS
AT THE
SAME TIME?

*Yes, try bartering
goods and services.*

Swapping one product or service
for another is a great way to avoid
cash outlays and unload slow-mov-
ing inventory.

Setting up barter relationships is
easy. You can directly approach
another business owner, or you can
hire a commissioned barter broker—check the Yellow Pages under
"Barter" for leads. Or join a barter
club or exchange.

Bartering can be particularly
useful for service entrepreneurs,
who can easily swap their skills with
other service providers. Or you can
barter for benefits with a local den-
tist or doctor.

Remember, though, the IRS considers bartered goods and services
taxable, so keep track of everything
you do.

IN SEVERE HIRING CRUNCHES, ENTREPRENEURS ARE OFTEN TEMPTED TO HIRE A FORMER EMPLOYEE.

But before you make that leap, consider the pros and cons.

On the plus side, by rehiring a former worker, you probably can reduce the risk of making a mistake. You know the employee's skills, abilities and work style. You know the person, and he or she knows your system. All in all, it sounds great.

But wait! Carefully consider why the person left in the first place, what he or she has been doing in the meantime, and why he wants to return.

It is often tempting to rehire marginal employees just because you need the bodies, and it seems easier than searching from scratch. That's the wrong reason.

If you have other employees, check with them to see what they thought of the ex-staffer. You should also ask suppliers, vendors and customers for their opinions.

Sure, it makes sense to take a close look at ex-employees when you're hiring, but make sure you have all the facts first.

Before you try to collect, take into account the amount of the bill and the cost involved in collecting it.

Should you always try to collect outstanding bills? The surprising answer is no!

First, you need to calculate what your in-house collection steps cost. These include issuing past-due notices and making phone calls or personal visits. Then consider your margins and what your actual losses would be if you wrote off the invoice.

Now you can set some general guidelines. For instance, balances under a certain amount will get a set number of letters and calls before they're written off. Higher balances may merit stronger efforts, including using an outside service to collect.

A collection agency can help you determine the balances worth pursuing. Agencies typically get a percentage of what they collect, so they know when to make the extra effort.

Here's a shocker for most of you: You don't necessarily need inventory to take orders for your products.

Here are some tactics to drive sales without products:

- *Use a prototype.* Design a flier or brochure that describes your product; then approach catalogs, retailers, distributors and manufacturer's reps seeking orders. You can also exhibit your prototype at trade show—or even flea market—and take orders for future delivery.
- *Advertise or send out direct mail, and see how many orders you receive.* Make sure you offer customers an option to cancel the order if it can't be delivered within 30 days.
- *If possible, produce a small quantity of products made with low-volume production techniques.* Don't worry if this costs you a bit more. Consider it an investment that will tell you if you have a product worth selling. Then, if it works, you can increase your production schedule.

It's possible to get a professionally designed site that generates sales and enhances your company's image for about $2,000.

WISH YOU COULD LAUNCH A **W**EB SITE, BUT THINK YOU CAN'T AFFORD IT? **W**ELL, EVEN IF YOU DON'T DESIGN IT YOURSELF, CHANCES ARE YOU CAN.

To keep costs down, start small. Try a one- to five-page site that describes your business and lets people know how to contact you. Be sure your site tells visitors what's new or special about your product or service.

People expect more from Web advertising, so it helps to offer some value-added material. Try to update this information at least monthly. This keeps people coming back to your site and reminds them to patronize your business.

In addition to setup charges, be prepared to pay hosting fees ($15 to $50 a month) and the registration fee for your domain name (about $70 a year). Also, don't forget to set aside a percentage of your overall marketing budget to cover promoting and publicizing your site.

This is particularly true of new business owners, or when your company is financially hurting.

The biggest problem with over-selling is you're so busy talking that you're not listening to your customer's needs. You can actually talk your way out of a sale by offering the customer too much information.

Think about buying a computer. Often computer salespeople spend so much time discussing RAM and megahertz that they never answer the prospective customer's true questions and subsequently lose the sale.

So what's the answer? It's easy—shut up and listen. Ask customers questions about *their* needs, and keep asking until you figure out how you can fill those needs.

ARE YOU TOO PUSHY? MANY ENTREPRENEURS MISTAKE PUSH FOR PASSION AND OVERSELL THEIR GOODS OR SERVICES, TURNING OFF PROSPECTIVE CUSTOMERS.

It's often easier to land those first customers by knowing what you're looking for. Here are some smart ways to focus on your target market:

- Realize you don't—and can't—sell to everyone.
- Describe what you sell. And remember to emphasize how your product or service benefits customers.
- Determine why customers need your product or service and then match your business with those most likely to buy from you.
- Once you find your most-likely customers, target those most willing to pay your fees.

Finally, analyze where these targeted customers are, what they read and what events or trade shows they attend. In other words, once you find them, you have to tell or show them who you are and what you have to offer.

GETTING THOSE FIRST CUSTOMERS IS TOUGH. BUT REMEMBER, YOUR FIRST CLIENTS ARE NOT LIKELY TO BE YOUR IDEAL CUSTOMERS OR YOUR BIGGEST ACCOUNTS.

*Avoid these five common traps
so both your business and
your marriage can thrive.*

ARE YOU
CONSIDERING
STARTING A
BUSINESS WITH
YOUR SPOUSE?
WAIT!

1. *Misplacing your priorities:* Your relationship should always come first. Don't let the business become more important than the marriage.
2. *Overworking:* Don't fall into the all-work-and-no-play trap. It proves deadly to both the business and the relationship.
3. *Poor communication:* Couples must talk openly and frequently about both business and personal issues.
4. *Forgetting the big picture:* It's all too easy to get bogged down in daily minutia. But don't lose sight of your business or personal goals.
5. *Conflicting personalities:* In business, it's actually better to think differently than the same. Consider your differences opportunities to grow your business.

EVERY ENTREPRENEUR HAS—OR SHOULD HAVE—GOALS.

But do you know how to effectively accomplish them?

- *Put them in writing.* This sounds simple but is often the difference between goals that remain dreams and those that become accomplishments.
- *Challenge yourself.* Sure, you must always be true to yourself. But to reach new heights, you have to push beyond your previous limits.
- *Distinguish between long- and short-term goals.* Short-term goals are the building blocks for your long-term vision. They should not read like a to-do list.
- *Focus on the goal, not the journey.* It's too easy to lose sight of your goals when life has a nasty habit of interfering. Sometimes it helps to post your goals where you can see them often.
- *Be flexible about how you will achieve your goals.* Trust your intuition, and never expect for it to happen the "right" way.

IN MANY BUSINESSES, THE PHRASE "SATISFACTION GUARANTEED" IS AN OXYMORON. DON'T LET THAT HAPPEN TO YOUR BUSINESS.

You need to make sure the word "guarantee" really means something.

The most important part of a guarantee is not that it serves as a marketing tool but that it represents your customer service philosophy. Here's how to develop an effective guarantee:

First, review your past performance. If your business is doing well and you're satisfying your customers, then you're at little risk offering a guarantee. On the other hand, if you're losing market share or have recently received complaints, fix the problem before you extend a guarantee.

Make your guarantee direct and sincere. What you guarantee should be spelled out. Be accurate and specific, but don't drown customers in the small print.

Finally, your guarantee should be easy to implement. And don't forget to promote it. Place it prominently in your office and on your brochures, packages and invoices.

*Here are some smart ways
to capitalize on your
business cards:*

ARE YOU
USING YOUR
BUSINESS CARDS?
I DON'T MEAN
ARE YOU
HANDING
THEM OUT,
BUT ARE YOU
USING THEM
TO YOUR BEST
ADVANTAGE?

Post your cards anywhere and everywhere they're allowed: Try libraries, college campuses, supermarkets and office supply stores for a start.

Get creative. Put your cards in unlikely places; just make sure your prospective clients are likely to find them.

Never pass up the chance to pass out your cards. Whether you're buying gas or groceries, if you think you've run into someone who can use, or refer, your business, give them your card.

Include your business card when you pay your bills, particularly your local ones. You never know if the person opening the mail might need your product or service.

Or, you can use other people's cards to grow your business. Contact a local business that's complimentary to yours, and ask if you can place a fishbowl on their counter. Ask customers to drop in a card for a chance to win a prize.

And ask as many questions as you can.

Study the financial records provided by the current business owner, but don't rely on them exclusively. Insist on seeing the tax returns for at least the past three years. Also, where applicable, ask for sales tax records.

Find out how the owner determined the asking price. With your accountant, decide whether the business's assets and expenses were realistically valued.

Who are the employees? If it's a family-run operation, salaries may be unrealistically low, resulting in a bottom line that's unrealistically high.

Will you need to change the business's image? If so, will the current inventory still be valuable to you? Also, will changing the image impact the existing customer base?

Whatever you do, don't go it alone. When you're buying a business, you need a good lawyer, accountant or expert advisor on your side.

CONSIDERING BUYING A BUSINESS RATHER THAN BUILDING ONE FROM SCRATCH? BEFORE YOU SIGN, CHECK THE BUSINESS'S NUMBERS

ARE YOU LOOKING FOR PEOPLE TO SELL YOUR GOODS? WHO YOU HIRE CAN MAKE A BIG DIFFERENCE IN HOW YOUR COMPANY GROWS.

Try these hiring tips:

- *Don't rely solely on resumes.* Good salespeople should be able to sell themselves without pieces of paper.
- *In the first phone contact, if the applicant doesn't ask for an appointment, stop right there.* If they won't ask for an interview now, they're not likely to ask for orders later.
- *Determine if the person sounds like someone you'd like to spend time with.* If not, it's probable your customers won't want to, either.
- *Pay attention to whether or not the applicant listens.* If the person is too busy talking to listen to you, he or she is not going to listen to your customers.
- *At the end of your phone call, say you plan to talk to other candidates.* If someone says "You don't need to talk to anyone; I'm your person," you may not need to look further.

WHAT WOULD HAPPEN IF YOU LOST REPORTS, PROPOSALS, PAYROLL, INVOICES OR YOUR CLIENT DATABASE? YOUR BUSINESS COULD COME TO A SCREECHING HALT.

Well, that could happen if you don't back up your computer files daily.

Your best bet is a tape-drive backup system. You can buy either an internal drive or an external unit for less than $500. All systems come with software to help you get set up.

Once you have a system, make sure you use it. Perform incremental backups daily and full backups weekly. Don't store all your documents in a single directory. Using individual folders makes it easier to recover lost files.

Use different tapes or disks for each backup. In other words, don't use the same tape on Tuesday that you used on Monday. And alternate your weekly tapes as well.

Store your backup tapes off-site if possible. If you can't, store them in a fireproof safe.

Eye fatigue is not entirely preventable, but you can avoid some of the strain by controlling your lighting conditions.

Experts say the ideal environment is an evenly lit, all-white room with no windows. While that may be hard to achieve, there are things you can do to improve your lighting.

HAVE YOU RUBBED YOUR EYES LATELY? THAT PROBABLY MEANS YOU HAVE TIRED EYES.

- Fluorescent lighting is a good light source. But make sure the light comes from more than one direction.
- Wall sconces direct light upward creating a uniform plane of brightness on the ceiling that then reflects down to the work surface.
- Torchier lamps evenly brighten rooms, improving reading conditions. Table lamps, on the other hand, should never be used as your only light source. They create patches of light and dark.

These suggestions might sound trivial, but most experts believe up to 95 percent of all home offices have the wrong lighting.

Protect yourself.

Whether you are approached over the phone or by mail, you should scrutinize all solicitations before making any agreements or purchasing any merchandise. You should also:

SCAMS COME IN MANY FORMS, AND THOSE TARGETING SMALL-BUSINESS OWNERS SEEM TO BE MULTIPLYING.

- *Check all invoices.* Make sure the item for which you're being billed was authorized by you or an employee. Read the fine print to ensure the bill is what it seems to be.
- *Avoid saying too much over the phone to unknown callers.* Ask where the caller got your name and specifically what they are trying to sell you.
- *Always, always, always get references.* The more names on the list, the better.
- *Avoid being pressured into signing a contract.* Scammers depend on catching you off-guard, so don't get browbeaten into making a snap decision.

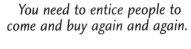

You need to entice people to come and buy again and again.

DON'T TREAT YOUR WEB STORE LIKE A VENDING MACHINE: FOLKS WON'T JUST STOP BY AND PUMP IN THE NICKELS.

- Get people to leave their names and e-mail addresses so you can keep them informed about sales, new product launches and more.
- Your sales copy should be short but snappy, and prices should be clearly marked.
- Use regular retail sales strategies. These include having sales, discounting items and offering coupons.
- Let your customers know who you are. List your fax and phone numbers, as well as your e-mail address. Customers want to know you can be easily contacted.
- Make sure you register your Web store with the top search engines. Or use a service that does this for you. After all, customers can't buy from you if they can't find you.

LIKE IT OR NOT, AT SOME POINT IN YOUR BUSINESS'S LIFE, YOU'RE LIKELY TO NEED AN ATTORNEY.

Once you hire a lawyer, you'll want to put him or her to the best use. Here's how:

If there's a problem, get your lawyer involved early. As attorney Mark Diener says, "A five-minute phone call can prevent five years of litigation." When in doubt, always check with your attorney first.

But don't waste your lawyer's time. Be prepared *before* you call. It's not only more efficient, but it will save you money.

Don't withhold information from your lawyer because you assume it's not significant. And don't tell him or her how to do the job. Your lawyer probably has better options than those you've thought of.

Finally, put your instructions in writing. And read—and correct when necessary—all correspondence from your attorney.

AS AN ENTREPRENEUR, YOU'LL PROBABLY HAVE TO WRITE HUNDREDS OF PITCH LETTERS.

Here's what not to include:

- *Overly solicitous greetings:* Try to stick with "Dear." It may not be original, but it's not silly or clichéd.
- *Exaggerations:* Don't send your prospects a snow job; you're sure to lose credibility if you do. Try to say something nice about the prospect's business, but strive to be believable.
- *Dramatic punctuation:* Don't overuse exclamation points, underlines, italics and bold typefaces. And limit your use of fonts; remember, it's a letter, not an ad.
- *Too much information:* Don't waste prospects' time giving them data they don't need. Tell prospects what you can do for them and why they should choose you instead of a competitor.
- *Odd closings:* Keep it simple, not desperate. You are, after all, trying to sound sincere.

Where else can you go?

SOMETIMES HOMEBASED ENTREPRENEURS NEED TO HOST A MEETING OR PRESENTATION, AND THE HOME OFFICE IS SIMPLY NOT APPROPRIATE.

There are more choices than ever for outside meeting sites. But make sure you plan ahead so you can find and reserve suitable space.

Many areas now have executive office clubs where you can rent a host of office facilities, including multimedia conference rooms and state-of-the-art computer equipment on an as-needed hourly basis.

If you can't find a club in your area, perhaps an executive office suite is the answer. Although most prefer long-term rentals, some offer daily or hourly rates.

Small hotels may have affordable meeting facilities for a small group. Call around and compare rates.

If you're meeting with people who are traveling, check out some of the airline clubs at your local airport. Most have excellent meeting rooms, though most require you to be a member before you use their facilities.

Which is best for you?

First, ask yourself two questions: 1) Am I willing to compromise in business decisions about my company? and 2) Do I feel comfortable trusting someone else to speak for me?

Before proceeding, remember you can be held legally liable for what your partner says and does. And don't look for a clone of yourself. You need someone with unique ideas and methods whom you can respect and work with as a team.

Once you find a prospective partner, make sure you define what each of you will be responsible for. Also, it's important that your commitment level and work ethics are similar, otherwise resentments can emerge.

When you're ready, put everything in writing. You can draw up the partnership agreement yourself, but I suggest you hire an attorney. Remember, your business is on the line, so make sure you include plans in case there's a split.

AT SOME POINT, MANY ENTREPRENEURS CONSIDER TAKING A PARTNER. WHILE THIS MAY BE SMART FOR SOME, FOR OTHERS IT'S BEST TO STAY SOLO.

Have you been to the library lately? Probably not, but you'll find some great reference books there to help you plan and run your business.

Here are just a few:

- *The Business Information Desk Reference: Where to Find Answers to Business Questions* tells you how to find information on almost any business topic.
- *The Encyclopedia of Business Information Sources* has 24,000 citations on more than 1,100 business subjects.
- *The Gale Directory of Publications and Broadcasting Media* is great for publicity hounds; it lists media by geographic area.
- *Standard and Poor's Industry Surveys* covers 69 major domestic industries and their future prospects.
- *The Thomas Register of American Manufacturers* is a comprehensive listing of all manufacturers nationwide.

If you have a problem finding any of these books, ask your librarian for assistance. You can find much of this information online as well.

CAN A
CONSULTANT
BOOST YOUR
BUSINESS?

Yes, if you choose wisely.

Before you hire a consultant, make sure you understand their role. Consultants are advisors, not miracle workers; generally they can't turn your business around overnight.

Still interested? OK, then first identify your needs. Write down specifically what you want to accomplish. Then tell the consultant what resources you're able to commit to help him or her do the job.

Prepare a list of questions to use when you're interviewing prospective consultants. And establish fees upfront. Some consultants charge flat rates; others bill by the hour, the day or the project.

Before you decide, ask for the names of at least three recent clients—and call them. Don't rely on letters of recommendation. If possible, talk to clients whose businesses are similar to yours.

Homebased entrepreneurs should take particular note of the following tips:

- Install and check surge protectors, smoke detectors, fire extinguishers, deadbolt locks and motion-sensitive outdoor lights.
- Keep your office equipment out of view from the street.
- Store all money and important documents in a fireproof safe.
- Develop a disaster recovery plan, and review it quarterly.
- Don't overload your electrical circuits.
- Keep stairs and walkways free of ice and debris.
- Set and enforce all safety rules.

For more information about crime, disaster and accident prevention, contact your insurance provider.

OF COURSE YOU NEED INSURANCE TO PROTECT YOUR BUSINESS FROM LOSSES. BUT THERE ARE SOME THINGS YOU CAN DO TO HELP PREVENT PROBLEMS.

But just because you're out of town doesn't mean you should abandon keeping fit. Try these tips:

BUSY ENTREPRENEURS OFTEN DON'T TAKE THE TIME WHILE TRAVELING TO STICK TO THEIR FITNESS PROGRAMS.

- *Walk whenever possible.* During breaks at meetings and conventions, take a walking break. Remember, you don't want to break out in a sweat; a brisk five- to 10-minute stroll should do.
- *Stretch for two to three minutes every hour or so.* You can even do a simple stretch routine while sitting in your chair.
- *Avoid sugar.* Sure, those sweet rolls, donuts and cookies often found at conferences taste great, but they only provide a short-term energy boost. In the long run, the sweets will act as a depressant.
- *Limit caffeine and alcohol.* These drinks dehydrate you and limit your ability to focus.
- *Drink water—lots of it.* Take a water bottle with you and fill it regularly.

Just follow these tips:

As a homebased business owner, you can't reclaim lost time, but you can keep it from escaping.

- *Avoid communication interruptions.* Telephone calls and e-mail messages can eat up valuable business time—if you allow them to constantly interrupt you. Set aside a specific time each day to return phone calls and e-mail. And remember, people are generally easier to reach right before lunch and at the end of the day.
- *Outsource some work.* Realize you can't possibly do it all, so stop trying. Look at what you do each day and determine if there are tasks someone else can do. If an accountant, assistant or consultant can make your life easier, hire one.
- *Establish regular office hours.* Do not allow yourself to be distracted by household responsibilities during work time.
- *Take a break.* Breaks let you get back to work with a fresh perspective and help you recharge your batteries.

YOU CAN TURN YOUR DREAMS INTO REALITY.

If you're ready to reach for the stars, here's how:

- *Visualize your future.* Write down the date you expect each of your goals to be accomplished. And then imagine you are there. When you write your goals, always use present tense, as in "My business *is* successful."
- *Stop beating yourself up.* We've all set goals we've failed to achieve. It's not the end of the world. Remember, failure is only truly a failure when you don't learn anything from it. As the gurus say "Businesses fail; people don't!"
- *Make sure your goals are dynamic, not static.* Your goals should be evolving; you need to constantly review and refine them. It's OK to change your goals; in fact, to truly grow, it's necessary to make modifications.
- *Have fun.* If you don't enjoy setting and achieving goals, then what's the point?

Here are some tips on how to maintain that professionalism:

JUST BECAUSE YOU'RE HOMEBASED DOESN'T MEAN YOU DON'T HAVE TO LOOK PROFESSIONAL. IF YOU'RE A HOMEBASED ENTREPRENEUR, IT'S EVEN MORE CRUCIAL.

- *Put it in writing.* Use letters of agreement and contracts for all your business transactions. This is not only professional, but eliminates the risk of misunderstandings.
- *Keep your marketing materials current.* Out-of-date materials make you look lazy and unprofessional. If you move, immediately print new materials and contact your entire client list.
- *Bank like a business, not a consumer.* As a business owner, you need a separate bank account and credit card. Develop a relationship with your banker—many are now courting entrepreneurs.

*Substance abusers can
negatively affect
a business's bottom line.*

E

EVEN IF YOU
ONLY HAVE
ONE EMPLOYEE,
YOU COULD BE
LOSING MONEY
IF THAT PERSON
HAS A DRUG
OR ALCOHOL
PROBLEM.

In fact, studies have shown substance abusers to be 33 percent to 50 percent less productive, and absent an average of three more weeks a year, than nonabusers. In addition, abusers claim nearly 400 percent more in medical benefits, file five times more workers' compensation suits and are accountable for 50 percent to 80 percent of workplace theft.

To shield their companies from these problems, many entrepreneurs are establishing substance-abuse prevention programs. An effective program should include a written policy that clearly states company expectations, practices and consequences, and an employee assistance plan.

There are a number of resources to help you create and implement a plan. Contact your local chamber of commerce or trade association for assistance.

CAN YOU
REPRODUCE
A CARTOON
FROM THE
DAILY PAPER
OR MAKE
50 COPIES OF A
MAGAZINE
ARTICLE TO USE
AT A MEETING?

Yes, but only if you get permission first. And that permission may cost you.

Cartoons and articles are considered intellectual property and are protected by a law designed to protect the intangible aspects of a business. In addition, a company's name, it's symbols or trademarks, items it has copyrighted or patented, and it's trade secrets are also protected.

Remember, this applies to your company as well, so make sure you have patented, trademarked, copyrighted or otherwise protected your intangible assets. If you're not sure what to do, check with your attorney or a lawyer who specializes in intellectual property issues.

And don't even think about using someone else's idea. Abuse of the law will cost you—and cost you big. Remember, now you're in business, too, and the golden rule—do unto others as you would have them do unto you—certainly applies.

*So before you knock
on anyone's door,
make sure you find out about:*

SMART
ENTREPRENEURS
DO NOT MAKE
SALES CALLS
WITHOUT
DOING THEIR
HOMEWORK.

- *The company:* How long has it been around? Is the founder still active in the business? Does the company or its owners support any of your favorite charities?
- *The folks you will be meeting with:* What do they do in the company? Who are the final decision makers?
- *Their comfort level:* How familiar are they with your product or service? Is this a first-time buy, or have they used something similar?
- *Their budget:* Is cost a factor? How flexible are they?
- *Any shared friends or suppliers:* Do you have any personal connections in common? You'll probably get a big boost if you were recommended by someone they know.

Remember, though, as prepared as you are, one visit probably won't seal the deal. Be persistent, and don't forget to follow up.

Here's how to set up your system:

When setting up a new account, call to find out what the business's payables procedures are. Ask if there's anything you can do to ensure prompt payment.

Make sure your invoice is easy to read and contains all the necessary information. Clearly identify your product or service, your terms and where to send payment. And don't forget the purchase order number.

Sometimes big companies pay certain bills on specific days of the month. Find out when checks for services like yours are cut so you don't miss the cycle.

Make sure you send your invoice to the right department. Does the company need the approval of the actual purchaser, or do they prefer you send your bill straight to accounting? Taking the time to refine your billing procedures could get you paid faster.

A SMART WAY TO IMPROVE YOUR CASH FLOW IS TO COORDINATE YOUR BILLING SYSTEM WITH YOUR CUSTOMERS' PAYABLES PROCEDURES.

Here are nine smart ways to give yourself the tech edge:

1. Fax or e-mail coupons or discount offers to prime customers.
2. Host an online forum or chat session with potential and existing clients.
3. Create a customer fax-request ordering system.
4. Use online advertising to reach people and markets previously beyond your geographical boundaries and your budget.
5. Create customer databases loaded with client information, including special dates, orders and preferences.
6. Check in on your competitor's Web sites regularly.
7. Be creative. Use graphic software to create fliers, brochures and newsletters.
8. Stay in touch—no matter where you are—with e-mail, pagers, cell phones and voice mail.
9. Post your message on as many free message boards as appropriate.

ARE YOU TAKING FULL ADVANTAGE OF TODAY'S TECHNOLOGY TO HELP MARKET YOUR BUSINESS?

*Here's what you need
to know to set up
an employee filing system:*

Create a general file for each worker, and make sure it contains his or her employment application, pre-hiring nonmedical testing materials, performance evaluations, salary changes, records of promotions or demotions, attendance records and any account of disciplinary action.

To protect employees' privacy, keep any medical information in a confidential file. Most states have laws regulating employees' rights to access their files. Although you may place some restrictions on this process, check with your attorney or state employment department.

This may sound like a lot of unnecessary paperwork, but properly maintained employee files can protect you from litigation, guide you when making promotion and compensation decisions, and help you run a more efficient business.

ALL BUSINESSES
HAVE ONE
THING IN
COMMON:
THEY MUST
KEEP
UP-TO-DATE
PERSONNEL
FILES.

But you can get the expert advice you need, and it won't cost you a fortune.

Computer resellers—or value-added resellers—increasingly view small businesses as an emerging market opportunity. Sound intriguing? Here's what to expect from a computer reseller:

Resellers are local, so they are accessible whenever you have questions about specific products or new technologies, or when you need tech support—fast! If you have industry-specific needs, your reseller can create customized hardware—and software solutions—just for you. In addition, resellers may provide preventive maintenance services, such as virus searches, regular support services, software training and hardware repair.

The best way to find a reseller is through referrals from friends, colleagues or business professionals like your accountant, banker or lawyer. Or contact a computer manufacturer for a list of local resellers specializing in their products.

MOST NEW ENTREPRENEURS ONLY DREAM ABOUT HAVING A FULL-TIME I.T. EXPERT TO SOLVE THEIR TECH NEEDS.

IF YOU'RE A HOMEBASED ENTREPRENEUR, CHANCES ARE YOU'RE BALANCING BUSINESS AND KIDS, AND THAT'S NO EASY TASK.

To help keep everyone happy, try these suggestions:

- Establish rules and boundaries—and keep them. Make sure your kids know your work is important and when it is appropriate to interrupt.
- Get your kids involved when it's possible and appropriate. They can help unpack boxes or attach labels and stamps.
- Create enough activities to keep them busy—and quiet. Set up a desk for them near, but not necessarily in your office, so they can play business while you do it for real.
- Hold a reading or writing contest to keep them quiet during work hours. Make sure the winner gets a fun reward.
- Take a 15-minute break every hour or two to check in with them and start them on a new activity.

*Increase your credibility
and your company's sales
by getting others to recognize
you as an expert.*

As a business owner, you've likely developed an expertise in your field.

First, choose your target market and then focus on the media they read or watch. Large national publications are not necessarily your best bet. Try the trade press, cable TV or local neighborhood newspapers.

Adapt your message to the media you're targeting. It's often better to concentrate on industry trends and news, instead of what's new with your business.

Send a pitch letter or press release. Make sure you start with a hook—something that will grab the reader's attention. Depending on your business, it often helps to include a photo. Follow up with a phone call.

Learn reporters' schedules and deadlines and work around them. Don't bother them during their busiest times.

Most important, be persistent. Remember, it takes time to build media relationships.

Paul Timm, from Brigham Young University's Marriott School of Management, uses the VISPAC method to stand out. Why not give it a try?

VISPAC stands for:

I IN TODAY'S INCREASINGLY COMPETITIVE ENVIRONMENT, IT'S IMPORTANT TO NOT ONLY MEET BUT BEAT YOUR CUSTOMERS' EXPECTATIONS.

- *Value:* Give customers a bit more than they expected for the price.
- *Information:* Provide additional information so customers can easily use your products and services.
- *Speed:* Never miss a promised deadline, and deliver early whenever possible.
- *Personality:* Make sure your company projects a friendly image. Greet your customers and always, always smile.
- *Add-on:* Give customers something extra. Try credits toward free merchandise, discounts on their next purchase or frequent buyer promotions.
- *Convenience:* Make it easy for folks to do business with you.

But there are ways to resist the temptation of the refrigerator.

Realize that your hunger is probably triggered by food cues, so it's important to eliminate these triggers. For instance, don't keep cookies on the counter or candy by the computer.

When you take a break, don't head for the kitchen. When possible, take a short walk outside. If you can't, try stretching or walking up and down the stairs for a few minutes.

Sure, it's tempting to "grab a quick lunch," but try to give yourself at least 30 minutes to savor your meal. Experts say you should never eat and work at the same time—but since I'm eating a sandwich as I write this, I'm not sure I can endorse that advice.

For many homebased entrepreneurs, food is company. So when that mood strikes, distract yourself by calling a friend or playing with a pet.

Follow these tips and hopefully the only thing that bulges will be your business's bottom line.

WEIGHT GAIN IS OFTEN AN OCCUPATIONAL HAZARD FOR NEW HOMEBASED ENTREPRENEURS.

REACHING PEOPLE BY E-MAIL IS STILL A RELATIVELY NEW MARKETING METHOD.

*Before you launch
an e-mail campaign,
keep these tips in mind:*

- *Get a good list.* List sources can be found in the Yellow Pages, in books or online. "Opt in" lists are lists of people who are interested in receiving information.
- *Keep your message short and concise.* E-mail readers want to know upfront what they're reading, or they won't bother to continue. Keep it to one screen length.
- *Be clear.* E-mail readers tend to be more suspicious. If your message is vague, it will quickly get deleted.
- *Get to the point.* Ask prospects to take some sort of action; this doesn't mean do a hard sell—just don't waste their time.
- *Start now!* E-mail still generates interest and curiosity, so get started before it becomes ordinary junk mail.

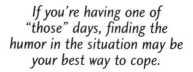

*If you're having one of
"those" days, finding the
humor in the situation may be
your best way to cope.*

The physical act of laughing
actually lifts our spirits, puts our
problems in perspective and
unleashes our creative energies. So
if you're not laughing enough, here
are some tips to get you started:

- *Take humor breaks.* Try a 15-
  minute break and read the
  comics, share a joke with a
  friend (or employee), or just
  draw funny pictures.
- *Surround yourself with happy
  people.* Don't spend all your
  time building your business; take
  time to enjoy life.
- *Create a humor kit.* Fill your kit
  with stuff that makes you
  laugh—cartoons, funny postcards, a comedy cassette. When
  you need a lift, dive into your
  kit.
- *Lighten up!* When things seem
  bleakest, ask yourself, how could
  this be worse? Your answers just
  may amuse you.

REMEMBER THE OLD ADAGE "LAUGHTER IS THE BEST MEDICINE"? WELL, THAT CERTAINLY APPLIES TO ENTREPRENEURS.

But don't give up; try these coping strategies when you need to tighten your belt:

FEELING CASH-CRUNCHED? THIS SITUATION HAPPENS MORE OFTEN THAN YOU'D GUESS TO MANY NEW ENTREPRENEURS.

Take on more work. This works particularly well if you're a home-based entrepreneur. You can get a part-time job or use a hobby to generate some quick cash. As long as you continue to serve your regular clients well, they won't know you're moonlighting.

Are there tasks you're currently outsourcing that you can do yourself? Or can you ask a friend, spouse, sibling or parent to help you out until the cash crunch passes?

Watch your expenses. Are there some places to cut corners without affecting the quality of your work? Take a close look at your phone bill, for instance. Are you paying for extras like call-forwarding or three-way calling that you rarely use?

Most important, maintain a positive attitude. If you keep working, it's likely the cash crisis will soon pass.

But most entrepreneurs don't do it right.

All ENTREPRENEURS KNOW GETTING REFERRALS FROM SATISFIED CLIENTS CAN BE THE KEY TO YOUR BUSINESS' SUCCESS.

Most ask for general referrals—Do you know anyone who might need my service?—rather than more specific ones like "Do you know someone who needs to upgrade their computer system?"

When getting a referral, try to gather as much information as possible. Ask your customers for permission to use their name when you contact their referrals. In fact, if possible ask your customers if they could help you get an appointment with their referrals.

Don't delay: Contact the referrals as soon as possible after learning their needs. And don't give up—even if they don't need your services at present, they may in the future.

Inform your customers as to the outcome of the contact with the referrals. And don't forget to send a handwritten thank-you note or appropriate token for their help.

Partners should complement one another—fill in each other's gaps.

CAN'T GO IT ALONE, OR SIMPLY DON'T WANT TO? THAT'S OK. JUST REMEMBER THE SEARCH FOR A BUSINESS PARTNER IS LIKE LOOKING FOR A SPOUSE.

If you're a great marketer, for instance, you should look for a partner who has a different set of talents and skills.

But like a marriage, you don't want to join forces with just anyone. Just like you wouldn't marry a stranger, you shouldn't hook up with one in business, either. As you pursue your partnership search, look for compatibility in work styles and attitudes, integrity, financial issues, and goals.

Partnerships should be beneficial for both parties. Make sure you consult a lawyer, and make your agreement legally binding. Even if your partner is a lifelong friend, relative or spouse, you never know what may happen. A legal agreement protects both sides and may ensure the relationship stays intact even if the business doesn't.

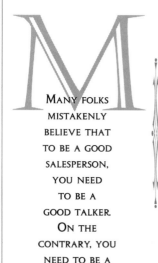

MANY FOLKS MISTAKENLY BELIEVE THAT TO BE A GOOD SALESPERSON, YOU NEED TO BE A GOOD TALKER. ON THE CONTRARY, YOU NEED TO BE A GOOD LISTENER.

This is not necessarily a difficult thing to do:

The hardest part is fighting your instinct to jabber away when you should be keeping your mouth closed and your ears open. Here are three smart tips to improve your listening skills:

- *Follow the 70/30 rule.* Listen 70 percent of the time, and talk the remaining 30 percent.
- *Don't interrupt.* It is usually tempting to interrupt because you feel you need to say something vitally important. Before you speak, ask yourself if what you're about to say is really necessary at that very moment.
- *Ask a question, and then shut up!* This forces you to listen. You can practice by pretending to be a TV interviewer.

Remember, the key to sales is finding out what your prospects problems are and *then* offering solutions. The best way—and the only way—to do that is to listen.

Try an employee leasing firm, or professional employer organization (PEO).

EVEN BUSINESS OWNERS WITH ONLY ONE EMPLOYEE CAN GIVE THEIR BUSINESSES A NEW LEASE ON LIFE.

With PEOs, you and/or all your employees become employees of the PEO. Your company then leases the employees back for a fee.

By using their collective clout, PEOs can provide insurance for small-business employees—insurance that might otherwise be unaffordable. The money you save on insurance costs alone could more than offset the PEO's fees.

Tasks like processing payroll and other administrative duties take entrepreneurs away from more important jobs like sales and marketing. PEOs take care of these administrative jobs.

Interested? You can look in your Yellow Pages under "Employment Services—Employee Leasing" for leads. But asking other small-business owners for recommendations is a better source. And, of course, check out any company before signing up.

IQ223

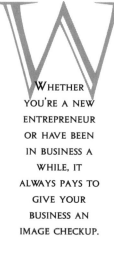

WHETHER YOU'RE A NEW ENTREPRENEUR OR HAVE BEEN IN BUSINESS A WHILE, IT ALWAYS PAYS TO GIVE YOUR BUSINESS AN IMAGE CHECKUP.

Professionalism is key, of course.

It starts with your company name. Is the name of your business descriptive and easily recognizable? If the name you started with isn't working, you can always change it.

Phone communication is vital, so make sure you (or your employees) answer the phone by clearly and distinctly stating your company name. Also, if you use an answering machine, the message should be short, upbeat and professional. Also, voice mail, available from your local phone company, often leaves a more professional impression than an answering machine.

Finally, what does your company do? Of course you know, but can you describe it in a single, clear sentence? Once you write this description, make sure you repeat it to all your prospects at networking events or on cold calls.

I

IN A TIGHT
JOB MARKET,
IT'S HARDER
THAN EVER FOR
ENTREPRENEURS
TO FIND
TOP-QUALITY
EMPLOYEES.

Sure, you can place an ad in the classifieds, but don't expect this to bring you the best job candidates. Here are some better techniques:

- *Tap into your personal and professional networks.* Tell everyone you know, from your vendors to your next-door neighbor, about your job opening.
- *Establish an employee referral program.* If you have employees, ask them to recommend people they know. Offer cash bonuses if the referral results in a hiring.
- *Contact school placement offices.* Include local colleges and universities, as well as trade and vocational schools.
- *Post notices at senior citizen centers.* Retirees needing extra income often make productive workers.
- *Use an employment agency.* The time you save in the search is probably worth the fee you'll pay.

OK, YOU'VE CONDUCTED ALL THE INTERVIEWS AND YOU'VE FOUND A JOB CANDIDATE YOU'D LIKE TO OFFER THE POSITION TO.

Now, how do you get the person to accept the job?

- Be sure your compensation package is competitive. Remember, salary is not necessarily the most important factor, so include as many perks as you can afford.
- People like to work where employees are positive, creative and happy. Would you want to work at your company?
- Treat the candidate with courtesy and respect. Just as you judge them in the interview, they are judging you.
- Introduce the candidate to current employees. This allows them to check out the folks they'll be working with.
- Always be on the lookout for good workers, even if you have no job openings. You never know when you will have to fill a position, and it's best to be prepared before you really have to be.

MORE AND MORE BUSINESS OWNERS ARE TAKING TO THE AIR WAVES—AS THE SPOKESPERSON FOR THEIR BUSINESSES ON RADIO AND TV.

Could you be next?
Before you hit the air,
consider the following:

- Remember, not everyone is cut out to be on the air. Some folks have weak voices; others may not photograph well. Get a brutally honest assessment of how you look and sound before you buy air time.
- If you need help, take a speech class at a local college. Or hire a coach to help you.
- Local TV or radio stations can help you prepare your spot. But first find out what your costs will be—remember, the ads need to be written and produced.
- If you're filming a TV spot, make sure you look good. Dress appropriately and get your hair and makeup professionally done.
- And finally, practice, practice, practice. You're not trying to be slick, but you should come across as professional. Most important, though, be yourself.

IQ227

ARE YOU A HOMEBASED ENTREPRENEUR WHO LONGS FOR THE RELATIVE PEACE AND QUIET OF A NOISY OFFICE?

Here are some ways to find harmony at home:

- *Scope out the sound levels in different parts of your home.* Are some spots quieter than others? Home offices away from the street and away from neighbors are your best bet. If available, basements or attics may provide the most privacy.
- *Talk to your neighbors.* Make them aware that you're working from home and that they may be unwittingly disturbing you. Most will make an attempt to quiet down.
- *Block the sound.* Open windows bring in the noise. Air conditioners or soothing music can block outside sounds.
- *Insulate your office.* If noise is a big problem, insulating your office may be worth the cost. Or you could do it yourself by hanging heavy fabric on the walls and windows.

AS A HOMEBASED BUSINESS OWNER, IT CAN BE HARD TO STAY FOCUSED ON THE TASK AT HAND: GROWING YOUR BUSINESS.

Follow these tips to keep you on the straight and narrow:

- *Set physical boundaries.* Clearly define your work space, and, if possible, close it off from the rest of the house. Insist that family members respect your work space.
- *Learn to manage your time.* Set goals, create to-do lists, establish priorities, and don't get distracted. Find an organizational system you like, and stick to it.
- *Create a mission statement.* Keep it to one or two sentences, and refer to it often.
- *Develop a growth plan.* Set targets for short- and long-term growth, and map out your strategy for reaching your goals.
- *Stop doing what doesn't work.* Often entrepreneurs continue bad behaviors because they don't know what else to do. It's critical you come up with alternatives.

FOR MANY BUSINESS OWNERS, "RECORD-KEEPING" IS A FOUR-LETTER WORD.

But it's essential to tame those paper and electronic piles to keep your business running smoothly.

It's easy for homebased entre-preneurs to let administrative tasks slide because there's so much to do and no one else to do it. But it's vital you keep your records up to date. There are a lot of good soft-ware packages on the market to help simplify the tasks. Check them out.

Also, make sure your computer files are in order. Back up critical data regularly and store it off-site. If this is impossible, keep it in a fireproof container.

YOU'RE NEVER TOO OLD TO STOP LEARNING.

*If you're learning,
you're growing—
and that translates
to a better business.*

If you need to brush up on your business skills or learn some new ones, it pays to make the time to go back to school. Check out the schedule of adult education classes at your local university, college or community unified school district. Then hit the books!

Another way to learn the ropes is to surround yourself with those in the know. Assemble a team of advisors, such as accountants, lawyers or expert marketers, to help you grow. Depending on your situation, your board could be paid—or if you know them well, be volunteers.

I IF YOU'RE ONE OF THE MILLIONS OF FOLKS SURFING THE NET, YOU MAY WONDER HOW TO MAKE SURE THE INFORMATION IS RELIABLE.

*Here are a few tips
to help weed the bad
from the good Web sites:*

- *Go straight to the source.* If
  you're seeking information about
  a particular company or it's
  products, try the business's own
  site or a site you know to be
  reliable first.
- *Use several search engines to
  research your topic.* Sites that
  appear in more than one search
  are more likely to be credible.
- *Consider the purpose of the
  site.* If it's advertising, understand the information is there to
  help sell products or services,
  and not necessarily to provide
  complete and thorough information.
- *Look for sites with tons of contact information.* It's easier for
  dishonest people to hide behind
  one e-mail address.

Remember, there's an incredible
amount of information on the Web.
Taking some precautions helps
ensure your searches yield positive
results.

But it's important that clients be able to reach you when they need you. Here's how to remain as accessible as possible:

I
IF YOU'RE LIKE
MANY
HOMEBASED
ENTREPRENEURS,
YOU DON'T
HAVE A
TRADITIONAL
OFFICE SETUP IN
WHICH CLIENTS
CAN REACH YOU
SIMPLY BY
WALKING IN THE
FRONT DOOR.

- *Maintain an up-to-date phone system.* Review your communications system at least once a year. Telecommunications technology is advancing so quickly, it's hard to keep up. Call several phone companies and compare how they can serve your needs.
- *Get connected with a reliable voice messaging system and/or a cell phone and pager.* Remember, busy signals are unprofessional, so make sure calls are forwarded to an answering system if you're on the line.
- *Consider—strongly— creating a Web site.* A site can help establish your presence in the market, provide existing and potential clients with information about your business and send the message that you are a forward-thinking company.

What do you do with unhappy customers? The way you answer that question could determine whether you keep customers or lose them.

Here's what to do:

Make sure you listen actively. Don't interrupt or show any emotion. Just listen. Once they've vented, they're more apt to listen to you.

Be kind. Plain talk and a steady voice are invaluable when handling a conflict. Sometimes it pays to give the customer the benefit of the doubt—you'll have to decide on a case-by-case basis.

When you're under verbal attack, don't blurt out the first words that come to mind. Instead, say "I'd like to hear what you have to say, but please slow down a bit so I can hear you." Or you can defuse the situation by saying "You talk first, and I won't interrupt. Then when you're done, I'll see if I have any questions." However you handle it, it's important to remain calm and try a little kindness.

If you think your business is too small—or too young—to commemorate the occasion, you're wrong.

N HAPPY ANNIVERSARY! IT'S AMAZING HOW MANY ENTREPRENEURS DON'T TAKE ADVANTAGE OF THEIR ANNIVERSARIES.

In fact, all businesses should acknowledge the special occasion somehow. It's basically a matter of deciding what you hope to accomplish.

Your celebration can target customers, employees, the local community or all of the above. Any occasion that gives you an additional reason to be in front of your clients is, as Martha Stewart says, a good thing.

How do you celebrate? You can throw an anniversary party and invite existing and promising potential clients. A more low-key approach is to offer a discount on future purchases.

Or you could take the altruistic approach and donate money to a local charity or good cause.

If you're thinking about starting your own support group so you have people to run ideas by and commiserate with, here's how:

THE WORLD IS FULL OF SUPPORT GROUPS, SO YOU MAY THINK "WHO NEEDS ANOTHER ONE?" HOMEBASED BUSINESS OWNERS, THAT'S WHO.

First, invite everyone you know who fits the profile of a prospective member. Realize your first meeting will likely be small, but membership should grow as the word gets around.

It's important to stay flexible. Some groups meet on set dates; others hold them open. Sometimes topics are set in advance, but more typically the group will gravitate to the topics they need to discuss.

Being part of a group can pay off in more than support. Join together and take advantage of group discounts and buying power. You may even end up partnering with some members of your group for business projects.

*You can now display the
Better Business Bureau seal
on your site.*

**DO YOU HAVE
AN ONLINE
BUSINESS?**

To obtain authorization, companies must be members of their local Better Business Bureau, provide information about their ownership and management, agree to an on-site inspection, have a satisfactory complaint-handling record from the bureau, promise to respond quickly to customer complaints, and agree to arbitration to resolve any issues regarding their online practices.

Customers visiting your site can click on the seal that verifies your participation in the program and provides additional information about your company.

As online commerce increases, customers are seeking assurances they won't be cheated. The Better Business Bureau seal may serve such a purpose. For more information, contact the bureau at bbbonline.org.

But sometimes "no" is the only thing you can say.

Try these tips the next time you've got to let a customer down easy:

First, realize saying no is not always bad. Focus on the strength of your relationship with the client, not on this one sale at this particular point in time. Remember, you're not necessarily doing what's best for your clients by always saying yes.

When you must say no, tell your client why, and be sure to offer alternatives. If, for example, you can't meet the requested deadline, say when you could get it done. If that's not acceptable, refer the client to someone who can get it done on time.

It's important your employees, if you have any, understand that it's better to turn down business than complete a mediocre job. If you're honest with your clients, most will understand your temporary refusal, and you'll preserve your relationship.

BUSY ENTREPRENEURS KNOW SOMETIMES IT IS BETTER TO "JUST SAY NO" BUT ARE AFRAID THAT SAYING NO TO A CLIENT WILL COST THEM A VALUED CUSTOMER.

Here's how:

- *Use your business cards.* Give your cards to everyone you meet—even if it's not a business situation. And make sure those cards accurately reflect your business's image.
- *Join the right associations and organizations.* Look for groups your prospects belong to, and concentrate your time there. And don't forget your industry trade group and local chamber of commerce.
- *Develop an elevator introduction.* You should be able to clearly describe what you do in 10 to 15 seconds. Practice until you get it right.
- *Use testimonials.* Nothing sells your business better than satisfied clients. Let them do the talking for you.

IF NO ONE KNOWS ABOUT YOUR BUSINESS, YOU'RE NOT GOING TO GROW ANYWHERE. SO SPREAD THE WORD.

That's a good time to develop a calendar to plan next year's marketing efforts.

WHEN IT STARTS TO LOOK A LOT LIKE CHRISTMAS, NEW YEAR'S IS RIGHT AROUND THE CORNER.

New Year's is the time to budget for specific marketing expenditures—Yellow Pages ads, cable TV promotions, newspaper inserts. But always set aside an extra 3 percent or 4 percent of your budget for unexpected marketing opportunities.

Give yourself plenty of time to plot your promotions. For instance, if you're staging a summer sale, you may need to start working on your plan in March.

Don't blindly schedule holiday promotions. They must be relevant to your business. Halloween decorations are fun in a kids' store but might be inappropriate in an accountant's office.

Above all, when you plan your marketing efforts, be flexible. Keep your eyes open for new opportunities to strut your stuff!

And many are sharing one space. But you don't have to be on each other's nerves. Here are some smart ways to avoid conflict:

O**NE OF THE NEWEST ENTREPRENEURIAL PHENOMENONS IS COUPLES RUNNING SEPARATE BUSINESSES OUT OF THEIR HOMES.**

- *Use any and all available technology.* Try virtual assistants, e-mail, cordless headsets and voice mail to solve privacy problems.
- *Live by the rule "separate but equal."* When setting up your work space, use partitions, and make it as soundproof as possible.
- *Share and share alike.* You can both use the same conference space, fax machine, copier or even printer. However, you should not share a phone.
- *Respect each other's responsibilities.* Don't expect your partner to set aside their business commitments to fix your computer, help with your mailing, etc.
- *Communicate regularly about your schedules, both verbally and in writing.* A calendar you both refer to can be a life—and relationship—saver.

Appropriate colors can make your work environment more comfortable and productive. Inappropriate colors can be distracting and increase anxiety.

So how do you choose the right color? Well, first remember that no color conveys the same feelings to everyone. But there are some common perceptions:

AT SOME POINT, ALMOST ALL ENTREPRENEURS CAN USE A LIFT—AND ONE OF THE BEST WAYS TO GET IT IS BY PAINTING YOUR OFFICE WALLS.

- Reds, oranges and yellows say earthy, friendly and approachable.
- Dark blue is refined, authoritative and classic.
- Blue-greens are more relaxing than yellow-greens.
- Bright colors are also energetic and enthusiastic, while muted shades are more conservative, casual and demure.
- Light colors are considered friendly, casual and feminine. Dark hues are dramatic, authoritative and masculine.

Don't struggle with this. Experiment with different colors. As long as you feel good, you'll be creative and productive.

*Etiquette expert
Letitia Baldridge shares
some sage advice:*

GIVING BUSINESS GIFTS CAN BE A SMART WAY TO CEMENT YOUR CUSTOMER RELATIONSHIPS. BUT IT'S NOT AS EASY AS IT SOUNDS.

Whether it's a personalized gift or a promotional token, the item should have some value to your customers.

If the gift is more personal in nature, remember the more you keep the recipient in mind, the more thoughtful the gesture.

It is important that promotional gifts convey a professional image. Don't give away shoddily designed or manufactured goods. The items needn't be expensive, but they should never look cheap.

Promotional gifts bearing your company's logo are often trickier. Unless your name is Calvin Klein or Tommy Hilfiger, keep the logo small and unobtrusive. This is especially true if the gifts are made to be displayed on a desk or carried in a briefcase.

*As you grow your business,
it's important to meet
as many people and learn
as much as you can.*

IT'S ESSENTIAL FOR ENTREPRENEURS TO GO TO AS MANY SEMINARS AND CONVENTIONS AS POSSIBLE.

With that in mind, here are some hints that can help you through your next event:

- Don't smoke unless other people are.
- Be enthusiastic and positive. Don't grumble, complain or lament your bad day. People want to do business with winners, not whiners.
- If you don't know anyone, stand in the food line. You'll be surrounded by people you can start talking to.
- Stay as late as you can. The longer you stay, the more contacts you can make.

Stop!

Before you make an offer, consider this: Nearly 25 percent of all resumes include some false information. Follow these steps to make sure you're hiring smart:

YOU'RE READY TO HIRE YOUR FIRST EMPLOYEE AND YOU'VE FOUND THE PERFECT PERSON.

- Get the applicant's signed authorization to allow former employers to release employment information. This is usually included in the job application.
- Verify education, former jobs and prior job responsibilities with the listed institutions and employers.
- Use credit checks when personal financial conduct is relevant—in retail jobs, for instance. You must get the applicant's written permission and provide copies of the credit report to the prospective employee *before* you take any adverse reaction based on the report.

*Here's how to find one
that best suits your needs.*

Different industries have different needs. Make sure the reps or agencies you talk to have experience in your field.

Visit stores you think might be interested in selling your products. Do they sell similar items? Then contact the store buyer and ask if they prefer to deal directly with the manufacturer—that's you—or with reps.

Ask other reps and manufacturers if they can recommend someone with expertise in your area. Or try the *MANA Directory*, a complete guide to manufacturer's reps, found in most large libraries.

Attend trade shows. You can often find listings of reps there, and at some shows you can actually meet them. However, before you go, make sure you know exactly what you want from a rep and delineate what you're offering.

ENTREPRENEURIAL INVENTORS OFTEN NEED TO FIND INDEPENDENT SALES REPS TO SELL THEIR GOODS.

ALL ENTREPRENEURS ARE TIME-CRUNCHED. BUT FOR HOMEBASED BUSINESS OWNERS, IT SEEMS LIKE FINDING TIME IS EVEN MORE DIFFICULT.

Try these time-saving tips:

- *Pool your projects.* Try scheduling meetings and errands on the same days to reduce the amount of time you spend out of the office.
- *Make the most of your downtime.* You can skim publications, catch up on your mail and make to-do lists while waiting in line at the bank or sitting in your doctor's office.
- *Use technology to save time.* Use mail-merge lists, macros, and templates and form letters when appropriate.
- *Most important, learn to delegate.* Ask your family for help on the homefront, and consider hiring a student to help with small office tasks.

No small business can thrive—or survive—if the owner doesn't promote it. This often seems imposing, but it needn't be.

Here are some smart promotional ideas:

Put other people to work for you by offering discounts and premiums to selected groups. Often, organizations will promote your business when you offer special deals to their members.

Always, always, always give out your business cards—even when you think it's not important. You never know who has relevant connections.

Get online. Create a site and promote it. This is more important than ever.

Start a referral program. Provide existing customers with incentives to refer friends and colleagues.

Finally, be visible in your community. Sponsor a sports team; be active in charitable events. Many entrepreneurs underestimate the value of serving their community.

As I've said, entrepreneurs often spend so much time worrying about finding new customers, they overlook their existing ones.

The following are six more quick tips to keeping your customers happy.

1. Continually stress the benefits, not the features, of your products or services.
2. Exceed your customer's expectations.
3. Don't focus on price. Point out the total value of your products.
4. Send thank-you notes to your customers expressing your appreciation for their continued business.
5. Ask customers for feedback— and then follow their advice.
6. Try to greet your customers by name, and remember some important information about them.

*Consider leasing
instead of buying.*

SHORT
ON CAPITAL
BUT LONG
ON EQUIPMENT
NEEDS?

By eliminating cash outlays
needed to buy equipment, leasing
frees up your money and helps
your cash flow.

Before you sign a leasing deal,
try to negotiate as much as you
can. Study the contract carefully.
Pay particular attention to the
terms, renewal options, equipment
value, payment amounts, cancellation penalties, and what happens to
the equipment at the end of the
lease.

Leasing is not a panacea. It usually costs more than buying out-
right. So why do it? Because leasing makes it possible to acquire
needed equipment you can't otherwise afford. And remember, whatever you lease for your business is
tax-deductible.

But these injuries are preventable.

The difficulties arise because the constant repetitive motion of keyboarding can damage nerves, joints, tendons, ligaments and other soft tissue. But there are some steps you can take to keep these problems at bay.

THERE IS A DOWNSIDE TO TECHNOLOGY— THE MORE WE USE COMPUTER KEYBOARDS, THE MORE SUSCEPTIBLE WE ARE TO REPETITIVE MOTION INJURIES.

- Before you start any intensive keyboarding, warm up by doing some simple stretches.
- Take lots of breaks—five minutes off every hour should make a difference.
- Use the proper equipment; ergonomic accessories abound today. Make sure your chair and desk are correctly positioned and the area is well-lit. Many folks swear by split keyboards.
- Finally, remember what your mother told you, and sit up straight!

*Instead, treat it like
an important part of
your marketing arsenal.*

SO MANY
NEW BUSINESS
OWNERS
MAKE THE
SAME COSTLY
MISTAKE—THEY
TREAT THEIR
COMPANY
BROCHURE
LIKE A BASIC
INFORMATION
PIECE.

When used correctly, brochures can position your company against your competitors, communicate the benefits of your product or service, and motivate prospects to take action.

Brochures usually have only a matter of seconds to capture someone's interest. So make sure yours has a readable, eye-catching design and focuses on what the customer will receive rather than on what you do.

Use compelling headlines, subheads and photos, and always end with a call to action and your phone number. Remember, your brochure is your calling card. It doesn't have to cost you a fortune, but its content better be right on the money.

Many turn to temporary help services to get them out of a bind.

E EVERY ENTREPRENEUR NEEDS SOME HELP NOW AND AGAIN.

To get good temp help, you need a good agency. Make sure it's accredited, and ask for references from other small-business clients.

You'll also want to know how the service recruits its people and if employees are tested, trained and paid a fair wage. If not, you'll likely end up with people who simply aren't qualified.

Once you find a good temp service, make sure you tell the agency exactly what you need and how long you'll need it. Provide the temp firm with a detailed job description and a list of the skills you're seeking.

Above all, be realistic. Many entrepreneurs end up hiring their temp workers, so make sure you get what you need.

WHEN IS A GOOD PRODUCT A GOOD IDEA? OBVIOUSLY, WHEN THE ORDERS FLOOD IN. SO HOW DO YOU KNOW BEFORE YOU HIT THE MARKET?

Product expert Don Debelak says good products must satisfy five key criteria before they go to market.

- Is the product easy to distribute? Entrepreneurs need easy-to-penetrate distribution networks open to small companies.
- Is the technology simple? Most products go through several prototypes and product changes. The more complex the technology, the more expensive it is to get to market.
- Is the item unique? Store buyers and consumers tend to break brand loyalty only when faced with the new and different.
- Are the product's benefits obvious?
- Can the product be sold for four to five times its manufacturing cost? There are a lot of folks ahead of the inventor who need to be paid, so you need to make sure there's money left for you.

ARE YOU GIVING WISELY? CHARITABLE SCAMS TARGETING SMALL BUSINESSES ARE ON THE RISE.

Here are some tips for smart giving:

Don't just give because you're asked. Develop a plan with a set annual donation amount.

If you have employees, to avoid duplicate donations, make sure all requests go to one person.

Ask the charity lots of questions before you donate. How much of the money actually goes to the charity? Statements reading "All proceeds to benefit the charity" usually mean the charity only gets what remains after expenses, and that's usually not much.

Don't allow just anyone to place canisters or candy machines in your business. Do your research first. To find out if a charity is legit, call your local charity registration office and Better Business Bureau.

ARE YOU SPENDING TOO MUCH BUT NOT QUITE SURE WHERE YOUR MONEY GOES? IT MAY BE TIME TO TAKE STOCK.

Track your expenses carefully for a month or two to see where you can cut costs.

- Are your outside services too expensive? Try bartering some of your services in exchange.
- Do your office supplies cost too much? Check out discounters and wholesale suppliers instead of paying retail.
- How much money would you save if you switched long-distance carriers? Ask your current service to match any offers.
- Are you spending too much on repairs? It may be time for some new equipment. That'll save you in the long run.
- Do you pay bills the minute they come in the door? Unless you're getting a discount, why not wait until the due date?

It's your business card.

All business cards should contain the vitals: your name and title, your company's name, street and e-mail address, phone and fax numbers, and your logo. More information than this gets crowded and can detract from your professional image.

You can order your cards from a local printer from their business card catalogs. When ordering, keep these factors in mind:

As I SAID EARLIER, ONE OF THE MOST IMPORTANT ITEMS IN A NEW ENTREPRENEUR'S ARSENAL IS ALSO ONE OF THE SIMPLEST.

- *Weight:* Most business cards are printed on 80-pound cover stock.
- *Finish:* Of the three available, the smooth finish is the most popular.
- *Color:* Today, two-color cards dominate. Most catalogs offer from five to 15 standard colors to choose from.
- *Quantity:* Setup is what costs, so it generally pays to order more cards rather than fewer.

Remember, cards leave an impression—make sure yours is a good one.

*But, say the experts,
you can't ignore your sleep or
you'll end up in a vicious cycle:*

The more you stress, the less you sleep, and the less you sleep, the more you're stressed.

If this sounds like you, you need to make sleep part of your strategic planning. A good night's sleep helps maintain your good health and energy level, which can give you an edge in business.

Not everyone needs a solid eight hours a night. Determine how much you need to feel rested and at your best.

Can't get to sleep? Focus on the benefits of a good night's rest. Remind yourself you need to garner the energy and enthusiasm to accomplish your tasks.

Remember, your sleeping habits affect your business—either positively or negatively. And here's one case where if you snooze, you definitely won't lose.

WORKING 18-HOUR DAYS PUTS SLEEP ON THE BOTTOM OF MANY NEW ENTREPRENEURS' PRIORITY LISTS.

So whether you're looking for your first place or are moving up, here's a general checklist of factors to consider:

LOCATION, LOCATION, LOCATION. WE ALL KNOW HOW IMPORTANT A BUSINESS'S LOCATION IS TO ITS SUCCESS.

- Proximity to your customer base, suppliers and employees
- Affordable rent—watch out for hidden costs
- Available and affordable parking
- Ease of entry and exit
- Is the space functional for your needs?
- Utility costs—these can vary widely from city to city
- Accessible transportation
- Appearance of area, building or shopping center
- Growth potential of site
- Zoning regulations
- City's future plans for the area

The importance of each item will vary with the type of business, but make sure you get what you need for your company.

Here's how to fix the problem:

"OH, MY ACHING BACK!" IF THIS SOUNDS LIKE YOU, OR YOUR EMPLOYEES, YOUR OFFICE COULD BE AN ERGONOMIC DISASTER.

Get up from your desk and stretch about once an hour. Also, vary your positions from sitting to reclining to standing. Make sure you have the right chair. Features to look for include a five-pronged stand, adjustable seat and height, lumbar support, and adjustable arm rests.

Do your knees and legs comfortably fit under your desk? They should. It's also important to protect your eyes. Reduce glare by dimming the overhead lighting when you're at the computer. Use a desk lamp if you need additional light while reading. Adjust your monitor's height so it's at or below eye level. The screen should be no closer than 20 inches from your eyes.

These tips may sound trivial, but studies have shown people are more productive in ergonomically correct environments.

*You can design your site
yourself, but chances are
you'll need to find an
Internet service provider (ISP).*

Following are some questions to
ask prospective ISPs:

- *How much server space will I
  have?* You'll need to know if
  your use of graphics will be limited.
- *How much access will I have to
  my site?* This is especially
  important if you plan to update
  your site regularly.
- *What kind of tech support do
  you provide?* As a small-
  business owner without a support staff, you'll need all the
  help you can get.
- *How do you handle failures?*
  Make sure the ISP has a backup
  system in place.
- *How long have you been in business?* You need stability, so look
  for an ISP that's been around for
  a year or two.

I'VE SAID IT
BEFORE, AND
YOU'LL HEAR IT
AGAIN: YOUR
BUSINESS NEEDS
TO HAVE A WEB
SITE TO BE
COMPETITIVE.

ARE YOUR CUSTOMERS PAYING YOU ON TIME? DELAYS OF 60 TO 90 DAYS CAN CAUSE UNDUE HARDSHIPS FOR CASH-STRAPPED NEW BUSINESSES.

So how do you handle late-paying customers?

A good first step is to call and ask when the check was mailed. If it hasn't been sent, ask when the invoice is scheduled for payment. Your goal is to get a commitment to pay. If the customer won't agree to pay by a given date, find out why. Once you get a reason, end the call.

If you can't get a straight answer, consider your cash flow needs and options. How important is this account to you? Should you write off the loss this time and insist all future purchases be c.o.d.? Should you send a personal letter? Your relationship with the client will guide you.

If all else fails, turn the matter over to an attorney or collection agency.

*These tiny missives
can have a big impact
on your marketing plans.*

GOOD THINGS
COME IN SMALL
PACKAGES, AND
POSTCARDS ARE
NO EXCEPTION.

Postcards are easy and inexpensive to produce. You can even create your own for pennies apiece on your computer.

Think of your postcard as a miniature billboard—you need an attention-grabbing headline. Keep the body copy short and simple—only one idea per postcard.

Make sure you have an urgent call to action, and make it easy for customers to respond. Include your fax and phone numbers, and street, e-mail and Web site addresses.

But don't overcrowd the card. It is small, so use easy-to-read graphics.

As long as you stay within the U.S. Post Office's size requirements, postcards are the most efficient—and inexpensive—form of mail. Check out the USPS' Web site at www.usps.com.

*To be productive,
you need to make
efficient use of your space.*

Design your principal workplace
with you in the center. You should
be able to perform multiple tasks
with reasonable reach. Keep a small
amount of office supplies at hand,
and store the rest elsewhere.

Unless you store three-ring
binders or other large books, keep
your bookshelves to a depth of 8
inches. This frees up floor space.
The tops of filing cabinets can hold
printers and scanners, so there's no
need for extra furniture.

Use your walls. Shelves, hanging
files, phones, fans and lights can all
be affixed to your walls, instead of
using precious floor and desk
space. Above all, stay organized:
Once a week, make sure you take
time to put everything in its place.

READY TO SIGN A LEASE?

Before you do, ask yourself these questions:

- Does the lease state the square footage of your space?
- Must the landlord provide a detailed list of expenses to support rent increases?
- Do you have the right to audit the landlord's books and records?
- If your use of the building is "interrupted," does the lease define available remedies, such as rent abatement or cancellation?
- If the landlord doesn't make requested repairs, can you pay for them and deduct the cost from your rent?
- Does the lease define how disputes will be handled?

Before you sign your lease, make sure you get what you want. And remember, everything is negotiable.

THE TELEPHONE IS ONE OF THE MOST POWERFUL SALES TOOLS.

But new entrepreneurs need to learn to harness its power.

First, develop the right attitude. When you call, stay calm, collected, focused and confident.

Before you dial, get into a selling mind-set. Ask yourself "What does this prospect need from me?" Then write down all the positive things you can help this client achieve.

The more you think about how you're going to help the customer, the more excited you'll get. In your mind, imagine the prospects are friends coming to you for advice. This helps you maintain a friendly, relaxed tone of voice.

Finally, smile while you talk; it actually makes a difference. Remember, conveying a positive image over the phone makes your cold calls more effective.

Assessment doesn't need to be an arduous or complicated process.

YOU DON'T NEED TO WAIT FOR THE NEW YEAR TO ASSESS THE PAST AND PLAN FOR THE FUTURE. WHY NOT DO IT TODAY?

Simply look back on the past six months. Examine your successes—and your failures—and figure out what went right, or wrong.

A common mistake many entrepreneurs make is focusing on the hits and ignoring the misses. But you might learn a lot more from your flops. Think about what went wrong and how you might have been able to prevent it. Figure out how to avoid repeating those errors.

Analyzing your mistakes is perhaps the most crucial part of this process because you'll learn what *not* to do. Above all, don't beat yourself up. Remember, it's OK to make a mistake once; it's only foolish to make the same one twice.

YOU NEED TO MAKE YOUR WEB SITE AS EFFECTIVE AND USER-FRIENDLY AS POSSIBLE.

Why not take the time to critique your site?

It's crucial that visitors be able to easily navigate your site. A navigation bar on each page helps visitors move to other areas of your site without having to return to the home page.

Speaking of the home page, each page of your site should be linked to your home page. Again, the navigation bar should enable folks to get around.

Good sites are interactive. Make sure visitors have a way to let you know they've been there and give you feedback. Also, surfers are not patient. They don't like to wait for complicated graphics to appear, so don't design what you don't need.

Finally, look at the site through the eyes of a stranger, and ask yourself if it makes sense and targets the right audience.

All entrepreneurs worry about finding new customers and keeping existing ones. Smart ones also try to win back former clients.

Try these suggestions to find your "lost" customers:

- Develop a most-wanted list. You need to identify the smaller clients you've had and lost so you can target them.
- Find out why they left. If you hear "Your product or service was not what we expected," press for details. Was it product shortfalls or shoddy customer service? Another common reply is "We found another company we like better." Find out if that decision was based on price, selection or better service. Then come up with an appropriate response.
- Ask for another chance. If necessary, come up with a peace offering.
- Most important, once you win customers back, switch to a high-maintenance mode to make sure you keep them.

Sick-building syndrome is one of today's biggest health threats.

FEELING BAD LATELY? IT MIGHT NOT BE THE FLU; YOUR BUILDING COULD BE MAKING YOU SICK.

Are you a victim? Symptoms include headaches; eye, nose or throat irritation; dry cough; dry or itchy skin; dizziness; and nausea or fatigue.

It's nearly impossible to remove all contaminants, but increasing ventilation and air-cleaning may be effective. In fact, air cleaners are relatively inexpensive to install, typically running between $150 and $250 a unit.

Experts recommend you buy a high-efficiency unit that can change the air four to six times per hour. When shopping for a machine, consider the sound they make; some units are noisier than others.

Air cleaners can be found at department stores, home and building supply stores, and office supply stores. Many folks swear by them.

TRYING TO GET YOUR PRODUCTS INTO WAL-MART? HERE'S SOME ADVICE— STRAIGHT FROM THE NATION'S LARGEST RETAILER.

Before you approach Wal-Mart, you must answer the following questions:

- Where is the future growth in this market going to come from?
- How does your product help position Wal-Mart to take advantage of this growth? In other words, how can Wal-Mart gain market share and control costs?
- Who is your customer?
- What is the overall size of your market, and who is your competition?
- What is your competitive advantage?
- How will your product impact related ones already in Wal-Mart stores?

If you can answer these questions, getting your product into Wal-Mart may be easier than you think.

Here are some things to consider:

CHOOSING A JANITORIAL SERVICE SOUNDS EASY, BUT THE CLEANERS WILL BE IN YOUR FACILITY AFTER HOURS. SO CHOOSE A SERVICE THAT'S TRUSTWORTHY AND RELIABLE.

First, develop a list of specifications. List areas that need to be cleaned, and what you expect the service to do.

Next, you need to prepare a request for proposal, or RFP, to get bids from contractors who make it past your initial screening.

Ask for client and financial references, evidence of workers' comp and liability insurance, and details on the company's hiring practices.

Finally, develop a scoring system. Experts say the most important criteria are experience, price and references.

W HEN IT COMES
TO RAISING
MONEY, MANY
BUSINESS OWNERS
SKIP THE
PREPARATION
STAGE AND
LAUNCH RIGHT
INTO DIALING
FOR DOLLARS.
WRONG
APPROACH.

*Before you look for investors,
make sure you:*

- *write a business plan.* After you
  prepare the plan, write a two-
  page executive summary. This
  part will be well-read.
- *have your accountant prepare
  historical financial statements.*
  Investors like these prepared by
  an independent outside party.
- *line up your references.*
  Investors may want to talk to
  your suppliers, customers,
  potential partners or professional advisors.
- *figure out your sizzle.* When
  you're asked what you do, you
  want your answer to be clever
  and memorable.
- *meet and greet.* Once you've
  isolated your investor prospects,
  you'll want personal introduc-
  tions to as many as possible.

A recent study revealed that gray-haired men were perceived not only to be less vital than other men but also less proficient.

CONVENTIONAL THINKING SAYS MEN WITH GRAY HAIR LOOK DISTINGUISHED. WELL, THOSE OLD RULES MAY NOT HOLD ANYMORE.

Only 27 percent of gray-haired participants were deemed "very capable." But when the same men were shown with hair color, nearly 50 percent were given the same label.

These findings are significant to many small-business owners because, in the entrepreneurial world, image is often king. Image expert John Molloy says today's youth-oriented society values a youthful appearance. So having gray hair could negatively impact your business.

The solution? Well, as they used to say, only your hairdresser knows for sure.

AS THE GLOBE SHRINKS, MORE AND MORE SMART ENTREPRENEURS ARE PREPARING TO DO BUSINESS OVERSEAS. ARE YOU?

Then you'll want to avoid the four most common exporting mistakes.

1. *Failing to plan a strategy:* Small businesses are particularly vulnerable to this lack of planning. But remember, it's harder to solve problems after the fact.
2. *Chasing inquiries all over the world:* Patience is key to international marketing. Experts say to expand one nation at a time. And do your homework on each country you plan to do business in.
3. *Assuming that if it works in America, it will work anywhere:* Sales and marketing efforts need to be tailored to each country you're expanding to. You cannot ignore the cultural differences that shape each market.
4. *Assuming business will be conducted in English:* You should at least be familiar with the local language, and always take your own translator.

WHAT DO YOU DO IF SOMETHING BAD HAPPENS TO ONE OF YOUR EMPLOYEES? WELL, YOU CAN'T IGNORE IT, THAT'S FOR SURE.

Here are some suggestions for dealing with workers in crisis situations:

- *Tend to the affected individual.* Find out what he or she needs, and provide it. The solution could be as simple as moral support or offering assistance with logistical issues such as transportation or food.
- *Take care of your other employees.* Get everyone together, and let them talk about the situation. If the situation warrants it—and this would be more rare—consider grief counseling.
- *Keep everyone informed.* If the affected employee deals often with specific clients or vendors, let them know what happened.
- *Smooth the employee's transition back to work.* Some people don't know how to treat someone who has suffered a loss. It's important you help put everyone at ease. And remember, through this phase, be as patient and understanding as possible.

Do you have a life? You may quickly answer yes, but the truth is many entrepreneurs sacrifice their life for their business.

And that is not *a good thing.*

As you start and grow your business, you may think it's important to join every group and organization that seems relevant—*don't!* Too much networking can leave you over-tired, unfocused, and with no personal time.

The solution? You have to learn—and, yes, this is hard for start-up entrepreneurs—when and what to say no to. Begin by identifying the activities that will most benefit your business and those that will advance your mission; then say no to all the others.

The old adage was that the key to success was working long and hard. That's wrong! The true path to success is doing the right thing at the right time. Try it—and then get a life!

But first, you have to research how you're going to transport your goods. This is not necessarily as difficult as it may sound.

Shipping your products encompasses everything from preparing the proper documentation to negotiating carrier rates and complying with foreign trade requirements. This process can often be more easily managed if you hire an international freight forwarder.

Freight forwarders take care of the paperwork and getting the cargo from your place to its final destination. There are lots of forwarding companies out there. When comparing them, look for expertise, reputation, reaction and response times, and pricing.

Remember to choose wisely. Your forwarder acts as your agent and will be perceived as an extension of your business.

ARE YOU READY TO EXPLORE YOUR OVERSEAS OPTIONS? THAT'S GOOD BECAUSE GOING GLOBAL CAN HELP YOUR BUSINESS GROW ASTRONOMICALLY.

Try starting an intern program.

Seeking a creative—and affordable—solution to your staffing problems?

Where do you find good interns? Start by contacting your local colleges or universities. Many have internship programs.

To make sure both parties benefit, you must prepare properly. Start by writing down the specific job requirements. Then list what the intern will gain. Remember, this is a learning experience for them.

Contact the college in advance to find out their requirements. Some schools require that interns be paid, and all expect you to do some paperwork so the student can earn the proper credits.

Once you get inquiries, request resumes and interview the candidates as you would any job seeker. After you hire an intern, remember to train and supervise them. If you're lucky, your intern may turn out to be a great future permanent employee.

Here are some smart ways to create a winning image for your company:

MOST ENTREPRENEURS ARE AWARE THEY NEED TO MAKE A GOOD FIRST IMPRESSION, BUT DO YOU REALIZE YOUR BUSINESS NEEDS TO DO THE SAME?

- Greet everyone with a smile. Whenever anyone enters your shop or office, they should be welcomed with a cheerful greeting. And all your employees should look up to date and be well-groomed.
- Make sure your receptionist has a pleasant voice and is easy to understand. Also, everyone should treated like they are your most important client.
- Now this may sound obvious, but it's so important, it bears repeating: Make sure your office, shop, restaurant or whatever is spotlessly clean.
- All your marketing materials should look professional and reflect your business. They should also be clear and understandable. Remember, these could be the first things people see from your business. Make sure they want to see more.

Is your business a pain in the neck, literally? Many entrepreneurs experience all sorts of aches and pains they've never had before.

Before you come down with something serious, try these preventative measures:

- If you're a homebased entrepreneur (or if you just take home work at night), don't use your kitchen table as a computer workstation. The height simply isn't right for typing.
- Speaking of typing, if you do a lot of inputting, use a wrist rest.
- If you spend significant amounts of time on the phone, invest in a headset. This will alleviate shoulder and neck pain.
- Make sure your furniture, particularly your chair, is ergonomically designed. The possible additional cost is well worth the potential savings in downtime and medical bills.
- Take time during your day (or night) to take frequent breaks, and try some daily stretching and strengthening exercises to ward off recurring problems.

*If this sounds like you,
it may be time to hire
an accountant.*

Every year it seems like it's becoming increasingly difficult to keep up with constantly changing tax rules.

This is an important step, so you don't want to take it lightly. Ask other entrepreneurs, former co-workers or your banker for referrals. When interviewing candidates, make sure you find out if they're CPAs and licensed to practice in your state. Ask about their specialty. Do they have any experience serving businesses like yours? How small— or big—are their other clients?

You'll also want to get the names of some of their current clients, and make sure you call them for references.

Don't forget to ask how much time they're willing to spend with you and how much that's going to cost. When in doubt, ask—you don't want any surprises.

ONE OF ENTREPRENEURS' MOST COMMON COMPLAINTS IS THEY CAN'T FIND PROPERLY TRAINED EMPLOYEES. ONE SOLUTION IS TO DO ON-THE JOB TRAINING.

Here are some suggestions for starting a training program at your company:

- Determine your training goals, and make sure they are specific.
- Honestly assess your current training program, if you have one. Then identify the area, if any, that works well in your business, and try to duplicate those efforts.
- If you have any stand-out employees, enlist their aid in training others. And if they are going to be training others, it might help to send them to training themselves.
- Finally, the task may seem overwhelming, but on-the-job training is really four steps: tell, show, do and follow up.

HOMEBASED ENTREPRENEURS WITH KIDS CAN BE A RECIPE FOR DISASTER. HOW DO YOU MANAGE THIS TOUGH SITUATION? FIRST, SET THE GROUND RULES.

Here are some tips to help you get started:

- *Rule No. 1:* Tell your kids "This is your home, but it is also my office." That means the things that make the business run—computers, files, etc., are off-limits to them.
- *Rule No. 2:* If possible, set office hours. This lets your kids know when it's OK to disturb you without taking you away from your work.
- *Rule No. 3:* Establish rituals. Even if you don't leave the house, when you're set to go into your office, tell your kids "Bye. I'm leaving." And you can signal when you're ready for interruptions by saying "Hi. I'm back."
- *Rule No. 4:* This is the most important rule: Follow the other rules. They not only help you, but they help your kids draw the line between your workday and your home day.

I

IT'S PROBABLY NOT AT THE TOP OF YOUR SHOPPING LIST, BUT YOU NEED TO COMPARISON SHOP FOR THE BEST INSURANCE POLICY.

Here's how to get the best insurance deals:

First, it's essential to shop around. You may say you don't have the time, but you need to make time. Rates among insurance companies vary widely. Some will throw in extra coverages, so don't hesitate to negotiate.

When possible, combine your various coverages. Almost all insurance carriers offer discounts when they carry more than one of your policies.

Review the amount of coverage you can get and at what cost. Often, you can drastically reduce your liability coverage for a nominal fee.

Increase your deductibles. If you're willing to absorb a larger risk, your rates will decrease accordingly.

And don't forget to review your policies annually. As your business grows, your needs are sure to change. It's most important to make sure you're covered.

IQ285

*Here are some smart tips
to do it right:*

THE **W**EB CAN HELP YOU DO MORE THAN GET INFORMATION, SELL PRODUCTS AND LET PEOPLE KNOW YOU'RE THERE. IT CAN HELP YOU FIND EMPLOYEES AS WELL.

First, create a recruitment site—an online advertisement—and link it to a search engine like Yahoo! or Infoseek. Make sure you explain what the job is, your requirements and salary. You'll want people to know what they're applying for before they waste their time—and yours.

Then develop an online application. This makes it easier for job applicants to express interest. Once you find some candidates, proceed as you would with any job search. You'll want to see resumes, interview applicants and check references.

Stay in touch via e-mail with those folks you liked but didn't hire. Even if you have no positions open, e-mail can keep them interested in your company in case one opens.

No one really likes to make cold calls, but for most start-up entrepreneurs, they're a necessary evil.

Follow these smart steps to turn your cold calls into hot sales:

- *Analyze your feelings and realize fear is usually the anticipation of negative results.* So instead of thinking about possible rejection, think about the business you'll gain if you make the sale.
- *Develop a market focus.* Your calls are more likely to result in sales if you target folks who have an interest in your product or service—and the money to pay for it.
- *Don't sell your product or service; sell its benefits.* Show people what you can do for them, and they're more likely to buy.
- *Be a good listener.* In fact, listen more than you talk. This way, you'll learn what the prospect's needs really are and how you can fill them.
- *Learn to accept "no."* Not everyone wants what you're selling. Don't take the rejection personally—just make the next call.

IQ287

Do your employees call in with "the flu" a little too often?

Of course, some absenteeism is normal, but here's how to make sure it doesn't get out of control:

First, are you setting a good example? Make sure you get to work on time. When you leave the office, let your employees know when you'll be back and how you can be reached.

Look around your company. Are there good reasons someone might be shirking their job? Have you set unrealistic goals or created an unpleasant working environment?

Be responsive to your employees' needs. If they occasionally ask for personal time off or time to take care of family matters, grant their request if possible.

And be prepared. Establish a relationship with a temporary employment service in case of emergencies.

WHILE YOUR ADVERTISING MAY BE EFFECTIVE IN ATTRACTING NEW CUSTOMERS, YOU SHOULD TAKE A DIFFERENT APPROACH TO KEEPING THEM.

Try these smart customer satisfaction tips:

- *Use punch cards.* Every time customers frequent your business, punch a hole in a card you've given them. After 10 punches, their next purchase is free or at a substantial discount.
- *Give something away.* Promote new purchases by including a freebie with them. Have the promotion relate to your business. For instance, restaurant owners could give away a free glass of wine.
- *Stay in touch with loyal clients.* You could send a monthly or quarterly newsletter. Send thank-you notes in appreciation for their business or referrals.
- *Always give top-notch customer service.* Customers, whether they're right or not, usually think they are. Deal with any conflicts quickly and quietly.

STILL TRYING
TO GET THE
HANG OF
E-MAIL?
JOIN THE CLUB.

*Follow these suggestions for
more effective e-mailing.*

- When writing a message, leave
  the recipient field blank as long
  as possible. This prevents the
  accidental premature sending of
  your message.
- Most e-mail packages allow you
  to include the sender's original
  message in your reply. This helps
  remind the person of what
  you're replying to.
- If you have more than one e-mail
  account, try to have your mail
  forwarded to the account you
  use the most. This can save you
  considerable time.
- Answer your e-mail. Many companies don't. If you've told people they can get in touch with
  you via e-mail and you don't
  respond, you're making an
  unprofessional impression that
  will badly reflect on your business.

Now, here are some tips for hiring smart:

READY TO HIRE? FIRST, CALM DOWN; WE ALL KNOW IT CAN BE A FRIGHTENING PROCESS.

You should conduct at least two interviews with your top prospects. In the first round, determine if they have the qualifications you're seeking. In the second interview, tell them more about your company and your expectations of them. Ask questions that give them a chance to show you how they will perform on the job.

Where applicable, ask to see samples of their work. When the interview is over, tell them when they can expect to hear from you.

Consider all candidates carefully. Don't hire the least expensive person to save money. On the other hand, don't overhire, either. Hire the person you most believe has the skills and abilities you need today to help grow your company tomorrow.

After you hire, make sure you welcome the person to your company, and remember to train them well.

For start-up entrepreneurs, this is even more important.

So when starting out, remember, what your clients see is just as important as what they hear.

Start with a coordinated stationery package that includes two-color business cards, letterhead and matching envelopes. Your logo should look distinctive. Do it yourself with the help of software, or hire a graphic designer. Ask your printer for referrals to designers. For a lower-cost alternative, try hiring an art student. To maintain a consistent message, use your logo on all your printed materials.

ALL ENTREPRENEURS KNOW HOW IMPORTANT IMAGE IS TO CONVEYING A SENSE OF PROFESSIONALISM.

The next step is to create a company brochure that conveys that your company is solid, stable and professional. Check out your competitor's brochures for clues as to what works best in your market.

It's a good idea to print your forms, invoices, contracts and estimates on letterhead to further convey a consistent, professional image.

If this sounds like you, here are some smart tips to make sure you can run a weekend enterprise without running yourself ragged:

ARE YOU A WEEKEND WARRIOR? MANY START-UP ENTREPRENEURS BEGIN THEIR BUSINESSES PART TIME ON THE WEEKENDS.

First, evaluate your other time commitments. Do you have to shuttle your kids to Little League every Saturday? Do you use the weekend to visit your parents or run errands? Make sure you're ready to fit a business into your weekend hours.

Make sure you continually check in with your spouse and kids to make sure resentments don't build. Focus on the positive; talk about how you expect this to soon be a full-time business.

Remember, it's the weekend: You *must* make some time to be good to yourself. Sleep in an extra hour or treat yourself to a special meal, a movie or a ballgame every once in a while. If you don't, you'll soon resent your weekend business.

The key is to register your site with as many search engines as possible.

ARE YOU STRUGGLING TO GET PEOPLE TO YOUR WEB SITE? YOU'RE NOT ALONE; MANY ENTREPRENEURS ARE IN THE SAME BOAT.

Search engines essentially are databases used to find Web sites. Users key in words describing what they're looking for, and the search engine lists sites that match the description.

It's up to you to select as many descriptors as possible that characterize your business. Use the name of your product or service, the name of your industry, and, when appropriate, your geographical location. Then add relevant modifiers. Always use plurals, so Web surfers can find you whether they key in plural or singular words.

To register your site, visit the search engine you're targeting and click on the "add URL" button. A form will appear that you fill in. In a few weeks, you'll find out if your site is appropriate and if you've been approved.

Well, think again.

Do you think a digital camera is too extravagant for your needs?

Digital cameras, which record images on a floppy disk so they can be later manipulated with computer programs, can be a wise business investment.

Using digital cameras eliminates film processing costs and waiting time. The camera gives you the freedom to take pictures without worrying what the quality will be after you scan a traditional photo into the computer.

Digital cameras come in handy for marketing efforts. If you create brochures, pamphlets or catalogs, digital cameras ultimately save you time and money. Many use digital photos in their company's Web site or newsletter.

As with all technology, the cost of digital cameras is decreasing. Just a few years ago, buying a new camera would have cost in excess of $1,000. Today, expect to spend $500 to $600.

*People are so inundated
with voice mail today,
leaving a blah message
is likely to get you zapped.*

IF YOU THINK
THERE'S
NOTHING TO
THINK ABOUT
WHEN YOU
LEAVE A
VOICE-MAIL
MESSAGE,
THINK AGAIN.

Think of your voice-mail message as a 30-second selling opportunity—content is key. Write down what you want to say, practice your script, and then toss it away before you call. You want your message to sound spontaneous, unrehearsed and upbeat.

Of course, you need to say who you are and why you're calling—make sure you include a benefit to them—and leave your phone number, twice. Remember to speak slowly so they can write down your name and number.

If someone referred you to the company, mention the name of the person who referred you at the start of your message. As with all things, the more you practice, the more adept you'll be at leaving effective messages.

How? By teaming up with other entrepreneurs at the same stage you are.

To get the most out of this arrangement, create a team with varied talents, experience and resources.

For instance, if you're an interior designer, you might want to ally with a painter, furniture refinisher and an upholsterer.

When recruiting team members, look for the skills you need and attend chamber meetings, industry conferences or leads groups to find people.

Start out with small interactions. Meet once a month to build rapport. Once you land a project, make sure you clearly define each entrepreneur's role. Everyone should understand his or her expected contributions and compensation.

Entrepreneurial teams can be a very smart way to build your business—at no cost. And remember to start team-building *before* you land an account.

YOU CAN GROW YOUR BUSINESS WITHOUT HIRING STAFF OR USING INDEPENDENT CONTRACTORS.

Here's a quick list of who's expected to do what.

As the manufacturer, you are expected to:

- make a quality product.
- create a demand for your product through marketing efforts and provide the marketing materials.
- be able to fill all orders the distributor gets.
- offer incentives to the distributor's sales team.
- not undercut your distribution network. In other words, if a customer calls you directly, pass that call on to your distributor.
- provide technical support and customer service.

You should expect your distributor to:

- respond quickly when you pass on leads.
- store your products prior to sale.
- fill customers' orders quickly and accurately.
- help build a market for your products.

F
REQUENTLY, NEW PRODUCT ENTREPRENEURS DON'T FULLY UNDERSTAND THE ROLE THEY PLAY AND WHAT THEY SHOULD EXPECT FROM THEIR DISTRIBUTORS.

Do you want to be an entrepreneur someday?

Here are some smart tips from author Valerie Young on the best way to stop dreaming—and start doing.

- *Get the point of life.* It's short; if you don't do it *now*, when will you?
- *Get passionate.* Most successful businesses are built on the entrepreneur's passion.
- *Get a grip on "it."* Young says "it" is what scares you—and "it" is different for everyone. Understand that fear comes with the territory.
- *Get real.* Know that it isn't going to be easy.
- *Get informed.* Talk to people, join associations, and read everything relevant.
- *Get ready.* Set a target date, and create a plan to get you there.
- *Get support.* If you have a network, call on them. If you don't, create one.
- *Get going.* Do at least one thing a day to advance your plan.

Check out the following before you run into big problems.

Your sales may be up, but how are your profits? Is your company financially healthy?

Are your expenses too high? Are you spending more than you used to? Impressive offices and luxury cars may look good, but make sure your receivables are growing faster than your payables.

Are your expenses too low? This shows you're not reinvesting in your business. If you want to make money, you have to spend some.

How's your inventory? You shouldn't be making or buying more goods than you're selling.

How many clients do you have? If you're dependent on only one or two clients, diversify—fast!

What's your tax liability? Are you setting aside funds to pay your estimated quarterly taxes?

Have you raised your prices? Your prices should be keeping up with market levels and allow for rising costs.

If you're suffering from just one or two of these situations, you're likely doing OK. But if a lot of this sounds like you, you'd better take steps to get healthy—now!

MEETINGS—
EVERYONE
HATES THEM,
BUT YOU CAN'T
GROW YOUR
BUSINESS
WITHOUT THEM.

Here's how to prepare for an effective meeting with sales prospects:

- *Do your homework.* Find out what the prospects' needs are before you meet with them. Then make a list of all the ways your product or service can benefit them.
- *Set realistic goals.* Meeting costs can easily add up to hundreds of dollars. So make sure each meeting moves the prospects closer to a positive buying decision.
- *Prepare quality materials.* As I've said before, you need a coordinated package of professional-looking printed materials, including business cards, letterhead, brochures and other presentation tools. Make sure your materials not only look good but are also well-written.
- *Rehearse your presentation.* Practice how you'll use your materials, particularly if you're doing a computer presentation.

OK, YOU'RE A HOMEBASED BUSINESS OWNER, AND YOU'VE SET THE RULES FOR YOUR KIDS.

Most of the time, it all works out—but what about those times when it doesn't?

Let's say your official workday is over, and the phone rings. It's an important client, and you have to take the call. Here are some smart ways to handle this professionally:

- Get a cordless phone as an extension to your business line. When you enter the "home" part of your house, take the phone with you. If it rings, answer it and walk back to your work space. Let the kids know that when this happens, they should try to be quiet until you're out of earshot.

- If pandemonium is truly breaking lose, don't answer the phone. Let it go into voice mail and call back as soon as you can get away or get the situation under control.

- Understand it may not be easy, but if you train your kids to respect your time, space and need for concentration, both your work and family life will be infinitely easier.

How's your—umm—memory? Are you on top of things, or are you starting to forget what you easily used to remember?

Memory expert Harry Lorayne offers these memory-enhancing techniques:

- *Write it down.* Get your thoughts on paper or in your computer. Making lists allows you to focus on more important tasks and gives you a record of what you need to do.
- *Use technology.* Leave yourself voice-mail messages. Try a personal digital assistant to help you keep track of phone numbers, schedules and lists.
- *Use word associations.* This is particularly helpful if you forget names. Associate the name with something unrelated so one thing reminds you of another. For instance, Jack reminds you of your brother Jack because they're both big Yankees fans.
- *Listen carefully.* Perhaps you think your memory's slipping, while in reality, you simply weren't paying attention.
- *Relax.* Don't feel guilty when you forget. Once you relax, you'll likely jog your memory.

IQ303

Are you happy with your cell phone?

Before you answer that question, or if you're shopping for a new phone service, here's a checklist to guide you:

First, ask about your coverage area. Where can your phone be used? Is the service local, regional or national? Compare that to your needs. What are the additional charges, if any, for roaming? Don't pay for what you don't need.

What about the equipment? Is size a factor? Generally, the smaller the phone, the shorter the talk time between recharges.

Is the sound quality consistent throughout the country? Some phones sound great locally but weaken when roaming in certain areas.

Finally, examine the service contract. Look for the best combination of air time, monthly fee, additional-minute charges and contract length.

Do you CHARGE ENOUGH FOR YOUR PRODUCTS OR SERVICES? MANY NEW ENTREPRENEURS DON'T.

When setting ⌐
keep these tips

- *What's the going rate?* Find the acceptable rate in your industry, both the high and the low end. Ask colleagues, and check with your trade association. Average that rate with your experience and expertise.
- *Are you a recognized expert in your field, or are there only a few folks who do what you do?* If so, then you can charge more. However, the more competition you have, the more competitive your prices have to be.
- *How busy are you?* If you have more work than you can handle, it might be a good time to raise rates. Sure, you'll lose some business, but the business you keep will be more profitable.
- *How valuable are you to your clients and customers?* If you provide products or services essential to your clients, then you can probably charge more.

Here are some tips to help you write the most important part of an ad—the headline.

- *Offer a benefit.* Does your business save your customers money, time, energy or what? Tell readers immediately why they should be interested in what you're selling.
- *Remember, in most cases, the shorter the headline, the better.* In no case should the headline exceed 20 words.
- *Make your message simple.* The headline should focus on one benefit; address any others in the ad copy.
- *Know your market.* Target the headline to a specific audience. If it's too broad, it won't mean anything to anyone.
- *Avoid all capital letters.* They're harder to read. And avoid fancy typefaces—unless you're trying to make a point, don't use strange fonts.
- *Be provocative.* Make readers want to keep reading. Effective headlines grab attention and compel prospects to read on.

IN THE BEGINNING, MOST ENTREPRENEURS NOT ONLY RUN THEIR BUSINESSES BUT SERVE AS ADVERTISING COPYWRITERS AS WELL.

Is your desk a mess? This is a particular problem for homebased entrepreneurs, for whom space is usually at a premium.

Try these organizational tips from expert Lisa Kanarek:

- The only items on your desk should be the stuff you use regularly. Anything else is clutter.
- Stacking trays are good organizational tools, but in- and out-baskets only work if you clear your trays daily.
- If you're left-handed, keep your phone on the right side of your desk and vice versa, so you don't have to write over a phone cord
- Add shelves near your desk, and store items you use less often, like dictionaries, three-hole punches and extra supplies there.
- Use drawer dividers to organize the items in your desk. This saves you from having to hunt through messy drawers looking for the items you need.

And yes, for those who've seen my office, let me add one more item on this topic: Do as I say, not as I do.

Many entrepreneurs are underinsured. To adequately assess your risk exposure, ask yourself these questions:

I

INSURANCE IS ONE OF THOSE THINGS THAT YOU PROBABLY DON'T THINK ABOUT BUT SHOULD.

- What would it cost to replace your equipment and supplies and to recover your records in the event of a disaster?
- Do you work with clients' materials on-site that you'd have to replace if something happened to them?
- If you maintain an inventory, what is its dollar value?
- If you weren't able to operate your business for any length of time, what would it cost in lost revenue?
- Do clients visit your office?
- Do you take equipment to other locations, such as clients' offices, exhibits or on the road?
- Does your work leave you vulnerable to professional liability claims?
- Do your customers require you to carry certain levels of insurance?

Here's how:

- *Be observant.* Notice the "stuff" in the prospect's office, and talk about any mutual passions you have. These can range from sports memorabilia to photographs or even music.
- *Ask qualifying questions.* New business meetings aren't about pitching product. It's a conversation, where you get the opportunity to learn your prospect's needs and present your solutions for solving them.
- *Offer good solutions.* At the end of the meeting, summarize your solutions to their needs, and answer any final questions they may have.
- *Take action.* If you've prepared properly, it's now time to ask for what you want. If it's hard for you to close the deal, you may not have given the prospect sufficient reason to buy. If so, ask why. And tackle their objections so they feel comfortable making the deal.

YOU CAN PREPARE AND PREPARE FOR A MEETING WITH SALES PROSPECTS, BUT ALL THE PREPARATION IN THE WORLD WON'T HELP IF YOU CAN'T RUN THE MEETING LIKE A PRO.

Take it from me—it's not!

THOSE WHO DON'T DO IT OFTEN THINK THAT BUSINESS TRAVEL IS EXCITING AND GLAMOROUS.

I can't tell you how many times I've returned from yet another business trip with yet another broken suitcase. So before *you* head out on the road, make sure your luggage is up to the task.

Look for bags with heavy-duty stitching and zippers, metal buckles, padded handles and shoulder straps. The luggage should be constructed out of thick ballistic nylon, leather, or a combination of the two. And dark colors hide scuffs better than lighter shades.

Since you can hardly fly anywhere nonstop anymore, look for luggage with a good set of wheels and an extending handle. Make sure the size of the bag conforms with the stricter carry-on policies now being imposed by the airlines.

Learn from my experiences, and don't be cheap. Buy the best luggage you can afford—or suitcase shopping will become an annual event.

*Now here's the best way
to present your release.*

- Make sure your headline states a benefit. It should instantly communicate why your information is important to the publication's readers.
- A simple layout works best. Don't use "arty" typefaces that make your release hard to read. And keep it short—no reporter has time to read hundreds of words before they get to the point.
- Finally, unless you are instructed not to, follow up with a phone call. It's easy for your release to get lost in the shuffle.

Building media relationships takes time. Be patient, and you will reap the rewards.

WE ALL KNOW HOW IMPORTANT PRESS RELEASES ARE IN GETTING YOUR BUSINESS NOTICED.

NEW ENTREPRENEURS ARE OFTEN OVERWHELMED BY ALL THEY HAVE TO DO AND END UP PUTTING OFF UNPLEASANT OR UNINTERESTING TASKS.

If this sounds like you, try these tips to help you take action:

- *Get organized.* A cluttered workplace can be distracting, so get rid of what you don't need, and find a place for the stuff you use.
- *Get a head start.* Instead of waiting for Monday to plan your day or week, take some time on Sunday, when you're likely to be more relaxed, to set your schedule.
- *Prioritize.* Plan your time based on the importance, effort and duration of your tasks.
- *Know yourself.* Figure out when you are most creative and when you prefer to tackle the mundane. Then plan your day accordingly.
- *Do what you hate.* If possible, do the work you tend to avoid first. Once it's out of the way, your mind will be clearer, and you'll be eager to take on more.
- *Get in the habit.* If you pick an hour or so each week to clean up, you'll soon find yourself regularly under control.

PRINTING COSTS ARE ONE OF THOSE NECESSARY EVILS—IT'S AN UNAVOIDABLE EXPENSE. BUT DON'T PAY MORE THAN YOU HAVE TO.

Try these ways to spend smart:

- *Proof thoroughly—at least three times.* And never sign the proof until you're sure. If you've approved a "mistake," you'll have to pay the cost of reprinting.
- *Evaluate your forms.* Are they as efficient and functional as possible? Can you combine a few forms into one? Can your six-part form shrink to four parts?
- *Order smart.* Only print what you can use in a reasonable time. Ordering too much not only ties up your money, but you also risk your materials becoming obsolete.
- *Seek advice.* Ask your printer if there's anything you can do to reduce costs.

Finally, price should not be your sole criteria. Consider quality, consistency, service and support before you choose a printer.

But everyone needs a break, so here's how you can get outta town:

The first challenge is psychological; you've got to give yourself permission to go. Schedule your trip during your slowest time of the year.

Don't plan the trip yourself. If your traveling companions have more time, let them do it. If not, use a travel agent; that's what they're for.

If this is your first vacation since starting your business, start small with a three- or four-day weekend excursion. Will you need someone to cover for you? Ask a fellow entrepreneur, and make sure you return the favor.

Make sure you leave important phone numbers, and tell your "relief" how routine matters are handled. Also, explain what warrants an emergency phone call to you.

Finally, it's up to you whether to tell your clients or not. Often a brief voice-mail message suffices, and if it makes you feel better, check your messages every other day.

WHEN'S THE LAST TIME YOU TOOK A VACATION? I THOUGHT SO. HOMEBASED ENTREPRENEURS IN PARTICULAR ARE TOO OFTEN AFRAID TO TAKE TIME OFF.

YOU DON'T NEED A BIG BUDGET TO GET A LOT OF ATTENTION FOR YOUR BUSINESS.

Try these smart publicity pointers:

- *Write a column.* Approach your local newspaper, and offer to write a column—for free—on your area of expertise or about business in general.
- *Speak up.* Volunteer to talk to business, civic and educational groups. Again, speak about what you know best, but don't try to sell anything. Your growing reputation will take care of that.
- *Get personal.* Include a very short—one or two lines—personal message when you send out your literature.
- *Join up.* Find the groups that are important to you—the local chamber or industry association—and join. Then make sure you show up for meetings.
- *Be a good neighbor.* Sponsor a Little League team or donate time, money or goods to a local cause. A few hundred dollars can go a long way toward gaining good will.

Do you know when it's the right time to hire?

Ask yourself these questions, and see if you've waited too long:

- Are you turning down assignments because you don't have time to do them?
- Have you missed some deadlines? Are you satisfied with the work you're doing?
- Do you spend more than half your time on clerical tasks?
- Are you consistently working more than 10 hours a day, plus weekends?
- Are your family and friends complaining about your lack of attention or participation?
- Have you needed to hire a temp worker or subcontract out some assignments?
- Do you often feel stressed, overworked or overwhelmed? Is your health suffering?
- Have you wondered if your business is worth the effort?

If you answered yes to even a few of these questions, it's likely you have too much work for one person—and it's probably time to get help.

AT THE END OF EVERY YEAR, DO YOU WONDER IF YOU'LL END UP PAYING TOO MUCH IN TAXES?

CPA Sandy Botkin says many new entrepreneurs don't take full advantage of the tax laws. Try his tips:

- If you own two cars, alternate your use of each car from month to month.
- If you have children under age 18, you can hire them at fully deductible wages and owe no social security or federal employment taxes if your company is a sole proprietorship or a partnership in which both partners are parents of the children. But don't cheat—they must perform actual work for your business.
- You may remember that dry cleaning and laundry expenses during a business trip are deductible. But you can also deduct your first dry-cleaning bill after returning home—however, only for the clothes dirtied while traveling.

IQ317

*It's smart to plan for
these visits in advance
because the impression
you make will last a long time.*

DO YOU HAVE
BUSINESS
VISITORS
COMING FROM
OUT OF TOWN?

Whether or not you're paying
for the guest's accommodations,
check out the hotel carefully. Does
it offer the necessary amenities,
including business services, restaurants and airport shuttle service?

Find out in advance what's
expected of you. Will you be
expected to play the role of host
for the entire trip? The best
approach is to simply ask. Even if
they plan to spend time on their
own, make sure you tell them about
local attractions and events.

Will your guests be bringing
their spouses or family? Are you
expected to entertain or plan their
itinerary as well?

It's important, particularly, if
you're meeting these clients for the
first time, that you create the right
impression. Don't go overboard—
extravagance may make you look
irresponsible—but don't be cheap,
either.

Try these on for size:

NO MATTER
THE SIZE OF
YOUR BUSINESS,
SOMETIMES IT'S
SMART TO
ADAPT BIG-
BUSINESS
STRATEGIES TO
YOUR COMPANY.

- *Use organizational charts and job descriptions.* Even if you only have one employee, that person needs a detailed job description to do his or her best work.
- *Schedule regular staff meetings.* No matter how small your staff, the best way to keep everyone informed and on-task is to meet regularly.
- *Form an advisory group.* This could consist of friends, former colleagues, your accountant, lawyer or even banker. Make sure you meet regularly, and ask for their objective opinions and guidance.
- *Stay organized.* This is the best way to make sure things don't fall through the cracks.

Remember, large companies can often absorb mistakes that could devastate a smaller business, so it's imperative you work smart.

Here, the original guerrilla marketer, Jay Conrad Levinson, shares the traits of a great guerrilla.

A RE YOU A GUERRILLA ENTREPRENEUR?

- Guerrilla entrepreneurs, says Levinson, know the journey is the goal, but they know they are in charge of their businesses, not the other way around.
- Balance is important to guerrillas. They build some free time into their work schedules and respect those leisure hours as much as their work ones.
- Guerrilla entrepreneurs live in the present while remaining well aware of the past and enticed by the future.
- Do you have a plan? Smart guerrillas do—they know who they are, where they're going, and how they're going to get there. And they re-evaluate their plans regularly.
- Finally, Levinson says, guerrilla entrepreneurs are positive and upbeat. Sure, life may be unfair and problems always arise, but it helps to keep your perspective and sense of humor.

BRAINSTORMING SESSIONS CAN BOOST CREATIVITY. **B**UT TOO OFTEN FOLKS THINK IT'S A FREE-FORM PROCESS. **B**UT THE BEST FREE-THINKING COMES FROM HAVING A PLAN.

*Follow these rules,
and let the juices flow:*

- Before you start, make sure you define the problem or issue you're going to discuss.
- During the session, make sure someone writes down all ideas as they surface.
- Once you get started, everyone must suspend judgment. Reserve criticism for after the session.
- Encourage people to build on the ideas of others. Remember, few ideas have a single author.
- The idea is to push the enve-lope—invite unconventional thinking. In fact, often the wilder the idea, the better.

And don't sweat the details. During brainstorming, quantity is more important than quality.

Here's what to look for in a Web hosting service:

Your Web host should have the ability to download at least 1GB of data monthly. It should provide accurate tallies of the numbers of hits, visitors and link transfers your site gets. And a good Web host should experience very little downtime during peak business hours.

There are lots of Web site hosting services out there, but not all can provide the top-notch service you need. Talk to several hosts before you choose one. And once you've made your decision, don't hesitate to switch hosts if your service is not as promised. Many Net-preneurs switch Web site hosts several times before finding the perfect one.

YOU CAN HAVE THE GREATEST PRODUCT OR SERVICE IN THE WORLD TO SELL ON YOUR WEB SITE, BUT UNTIL YOU FIND A HOST FOR YOUR SITE, YOU CAN'T SELL ANYTHING.

But you should. Your logo influences the first impression people have of your business.

So whether you're already in business and need a logo checkup or are just starting out and designing your logo, remember these tips:

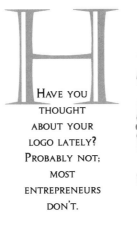

HAVE YOU THOUGHT ABOUT YOUR LOGO LATELY? PROBABLY NOT; MOST ENTREPRENEURS DON'T.

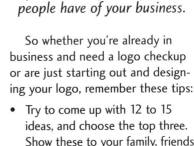

- Try to come up with 12 to 15 ideas, and choose the top three. Show these to your family, friends and colleagues before deciding.
- Make sure your logo appropriately conveys your business. Are you trying to portray a conservative, classy image or a funky one? Think about your target market—will they be attracted to your logo's font, color and overall design?
- Your logo should be easy to reproduce in a variety of sizes. Don't use a photograph; these often get fuzzy when duplicated.
- Once you choose a color for your logo, use it consistently. The more you stick with your image, the more people will remember it—and your business.

WRITING A BUSINESS PLAN IS A NECESSARY PROCESS FOR NEW ENTREPRENEURS, BUT IT NEEDN'T BE A SCARY ONE.

Here are some basic business plan suggestions to get you going:

The purpose of your plan is to not only help you raise money but to give you a road map. It should focus on marketing and financial information and explain how you intend to meet your goals.

Describe the members of your management team and what their titles and experience are. This area is particularly important to potential financiers.

In the market section of your plan, be sure to explain who your customers are and how they will benefit from your product or service. The financial section should have your projected profit and loss, cash flow and balance sheets.

Overall, keep the plan to less than 30 pages, and be sure to describe your product, your supplier relationships and your operations. Also mention plans for actions, growth and contingency.

EVEN IN THIS AGE OF VOICE MAIL, MANY BUSINESSES STILL NEED RECEPTIONISTS.

Before hiring a receptionist, heed these pointers:

Remember that the receptionist is the first person outsiders come into contact with in your business. So the impression your receptionist makes is vitally important.

The most important quality a receptionist needs is enthusiasm. This attitude conveys a lasting, positive impression.

Make sure your receptionist has a solid understanding of your company, what you do and how you're structured. This way, he or she can accurately direct customers to the person who can best help them.

When interviewing candidates, look for people who have initiative, ask questions and who have the patience and self-control to deal with difficult people. Once you hire the right receptionist, make sure you keep that person happy with a fair salary and treat him or her with respect.

To help you out of this quandary, here are some important questions to ask while you're shopping for a PC:

WITH MORE CHOICES THAN EVER, COMPUTER SHOPPING CAN BE CONFUSING.

- *What are the PC's basic components?* Find out about processor speed (start with no less than 233 MHz), memory (get as much as you can afford), and hard-drive size (you'll need a 3GB minimum). Also, you'll want to know what extras the PC comes with.
- *Is the machine upgradable?* The ability to install additional hard drives and memory will extend the life of your machine.
- *Does the machine come with a modem, and at what speed does it operate?* Is any special communications software part of the package?
- *What kind of service contract is available?* Ask what company offers the service and the basic contract terms, including length and type of service and the cost for buying additional services.

IN A RECENT SURVEY, ENTREPRENEURS COMPLAINED THAT ADMINISTRATIVE TASKS CONSUME TOO MUCH OF THEIR TIME.

Here are some smart ways to cut the time spent on these duties.

First, take an inventory of how you spend your time. List your activities, and keep the following in mind as you evaluate them:

- Be sure the task is essential. If it doesn't get done, will your business suffer?
- Can you systemize the task? By creating a step-by-step formula to get it done, you'll likely come up with the most efficient way to handle it.
- Delegate. Do you have a staff person to hand off the job to? If not, is it worth hiring a part-timer, a temp worker or outsourcing the work?
- If you decide to outsource, can you combine several related tasks and give yourself even more time?

It's important to remember time spent on trivial tasks takes time away from income-generation.

ARE YOU RUNNING AN ETHICAL COMPANY? A RECENT SURVEY OF WORKERS REVEALED MORE THAN HALF FELT PRESSURE TO ACT UNETHICALLY ON THE JOB.

Here are some suggestions for building an ethical business:

First, establish clear standards for ethical behavior, and lead by example. You cannot expect others to do as you say and not as you do.

Next, make the consequences of noncompliance known. Make sure employees know what will happen if they act unethically or illegally, and be consistent about enforcement of conduct policies.

Finally, offer help for those in need. Let employees know they can approach you with an ethical dilemma without fear of reprisal. Are there outside resources you can refer your employees to when they're stressed or under pressure?

Above all, be compassionate with those who make mistakes, and, if possible, help them move forward.

But the costs of attending can add up considerably, so before you go, ask yourself these questions:

ONE OF THE BEST METHODS FOR NEW ENTREPRENEURS TO MARKET THEIR WARES IS TO EXHIBIT AT TRADE SHOWS.

- *Have I set specific goals for participating in this show?* Make sure you know what you hope to accomplish at the show, including how many leads you need to get, how many sales you must generate, and how many connections you need to make.
- *Is this the right show to meet my needs?* You'll want to make sure the show audience fits the profile of your best customer. For example, if you only distribute regionally, is a national show a waste of time and money?
- *Am I ready for this show?* You should always market to attendees before you get there. Mail a flier, postcard or coupon to current customers and past show attendees. Your goal is to make it worth their while to stop by your booth.

*If you're planning
to serve alcohol
at your holiday festivities,
you might want to think again.*

Holiday
PARTIES ARE
SUPPOSED TO BE
FULL OF CHEER,
BUT SMART
ENTREPRENEURS
ARE ALERT TO
THE DANGERS
THE SEASON
CAN BRING.

Inebriated employees, vendors, suppliers or guests can cause problems by getting into arguments with one another or by making inappropriate comments or gestures. And if someone leaving your party is hurt or injures another, you could be held liable.

I'm not saying don't host a year-end party; just do it the smart way. If you insist on serving alcohol, make it a no-host bar, and make sure the bartender refuses service to those who have had too much to drink. Be sure to have lots of food on hand as well.

Put someone in charge of watching out for fellow partygoers. Offer to pay cab fare for those who are intoxicated. Even smarter would be to host a no-alcohol bash, perhaps early in the day, and give your employees the rest of the day off.

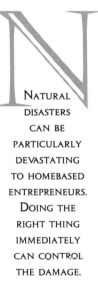

NATURAL DISASTERS CAN BE PARTICULARLY DEVASTATING TO HOMEBASED ENTREPRENEURS. DOING THE RIGHT THING IMMEDIATELY CAN CONTROL THE DAMAGE.

Follow these suggestions:

- Make sure it's safe to go back into your home. Be aware of hazards such as possible electrocution or collapsing walls, ceilings or floors.
- Contact your insurance company immediately. Then let employees, customers and suppliers know what happened.
- If the damage is so extensive that you can't work in your office, keep all receipts for temporary office space and related costs. Check your insurance policy to see if these expenses are covered.
- To speed up the claims process, take pictures of the damage
- Contact a professional restoration contractor to help you start recovering. Get bids from several before selecting one.

Come up with a disaster plan before you need one.

Heed these smart e-mail tips:

E-MAIL IS FAST BECOMING ONE OF THE BEST WAYS TO COMMUNICATE, BUT BE CAREFUL. USING IT THE WRONG WAY CAN HURT YOU AND YOUR BUSINESS.

Don't e-mail messages you don't want others to read. It is less private and secure than sending letters. In fact, copies often stay in the computer system long after you think you have deleted the message.

You don't want to be known as a "junk e-mailer," so be careful who you send your messages to. The more junk you send, the more you'll be ignored.

Keep your e-mail short. Most folks find it uncomfortable—and difficult—to read long messages on screen.

Finally, don't let e-mail take the place of personal contact. Many situations call for the more personal phone call or face-to-face meeting.

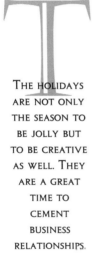

THE HOLIDAYS ARE NOT ONLY THE SEASON TO BE JOLLY BUT TO BE CREATIVE AS WELL. THEY ARE A GREAT TIME TO CEMENT BUSINESS RELATIONSHIPS.

Try these tips to get the most out of this holiday season:

- *Make a list—lots of them.* Make sure your card or gift list includes loyal clients, colleagues who've referred business to you, former customers you'd like to win back, and valuable employees.
- *Party on.* Be creative; you needn't spend a lot on a holiday bash. Rent an unusual location, such as a skating rink or a boat. Be sure to manage the alcohol intake of the partygoers.
- *Stand out in the crowd.* Your invitation or card will be one of many received by clients, so be creative. If you can't afford a professional, try hiring an art student to design your cards.
- *Deck the walls.* Help your employees and customers get in the mood by decorating your office or shop. Be sure you don't overdo it; you want festive, not gaudy.

Want more holiday tips? Turn the page.

WE JUST DISCUSSED FOUR SMART WAYS TO MAKE THE MOST OF YOUR HOLIDAY SEASON.

Here are four more:

- *Be card smart.* Your cards will stand out if you use a personal touch. Consider using a photo of your staff—it shows the real folks behind your business.
- *Give gifts that keep on giving.* Make a lasting impression by sending thoughtful, creative gifts rather than the standard food baskets or pen sets. Think about your clients' likes, and try tickets to a ballgame or show, or books about their hobbies and interests.
- *Remember, charity begins—well, you know where.* While money is always appreciated, you should think about donating time, products or services to worthy local causes. Encourage your employees to do the same.
- *Don't forget to say thanks.* Acknowledge invitations, cards and gifts. Make it personal, but be sure to remind them how your business will continue to meet their needs in the coming year.

Follow these smart tips to help you stand out from the pack:

One of the hardest tasks for new entrepreneurs is to distinguish themselves from the competition.

Don't try to be all things to all people; instead, be significant to a specific, targeted audience. This means knowing exactly who your customers are and what their wants and needs are.

Figure out your customers' dominant needs—that's the single most important reason why someone's going to use your product or service. This could be price, convenience or quality. Next, turn that need into a specific offer: What can your product or service do for them?

Once you define your primary customer base, carefully select the best markets in which to find them. Finally, don't try to grow too fast; that can destroy any business.

SELLING
PRODUCTS ON
THE INTERNET
IS ONE OF
TODAY'S
SMARTEST NEW
BUSINESS
STRATEGIES.

*Here's how you can be
a smart seller, too:*

- *Stay informed.* Technology is changing rapidly. To be successful, you must keep up with the hot sites, e-commerce info and smart promotion strategies.
- *Be patient.* Internet success rarely happens overnight. You need to promote your site. One smart way to do this is establish as many links as possible to other, more well-established sites.
- *Target your links.* Trade links with sites that support your business. Links won't cost you anything, but if they're not targeted, they won't help you grow.
- *Give something away.* If folks leave your site with something that cost them nothing, they're more likely to return and spend money. And free downloads build traffic at your linked sites.

*If you're hand is held high,
it's time for Brainstorming
Session Setup 101:*

According to the experts, the ideal size of your group should be from five to seven people. Fewer than five doesn't give you enough material to work with, while groups larger than seven have a hard time staying focused.

Hold your meeting in a place in which you won't be interrupted by phone calls or customers. Off-site is best so you won't be visibly surrounded by piles of work. But don't choose a site that's too stimulating that you won't be able to focus on the task at hand.

You'll need a room big enough to hold large sheets of paper or a white, erasable board to record your thoughts and ideas. Most important, brainstormers need to have fun. Humor and light-heartedness are essential to increasing creativity. If you can't set the proper atmosphere, hire a facilitator who can.

WHERE'S THE BEST PLACE IN WHICH TO HOLD BRAINSTORMING SESSIONS? RAISE YOUR HAND IF IT'S IN A RESTAURANT DURING THE NOON LUNCH-HOUR RUSH.

IQ337

Try these tips for getting your releases noticed:

NEW ENTREPRENEURS KNOW THEY HAVE TO SEND OUT PRESS RELEASES TO SPREAD THE WORD ABOUT THEIR BUSINESSES, BUT DO YOU KNOW HOW?

First, select the right media for your story. Create a press list of reputable media that target your market. Familiarize yourself with each publication on your list so you'll know what kind of information they use and how they present it.

When you mail your release, send it to a specific writer or editor. You can send your release by mail, fax or e-mail. Call the publication to find out who to send your message to and that person's preferred method of receipt.

Don't write in generalities. Make sure your release contains beneficial information that is new, different or trendy.

Here are a few helpful hints for truly "fine dining":

ARE YOU WASTING YOUR LUNCH HOUR BY MERELY EATING? INSTEAD, USE IT FOR LUNCH DATES WITH CURRENT CLIENTS OR POTENTIAL CUSTOMERS.

- Make it clear you are hosting the meal, but offer your guests a choice of dates and times.
- Chose a restaurant where you feel comfortable and the environment is conducive to doing business.
- Make reservations, and show up at least 15 minutes early so you can greet your guests.
- Don't jump into talking shop—wait until most of the meal is over.
- Let your guests order first, and follow their lead when you order. Also, don't order food that's difficult or messy to eat.
- Leave your cell phone at the office, or at least turn it off during the meal.
- Limit your intake of alcohol.
- Don't fuss over your order or hassle the server. You don't want to leave a bad impression.

MOST ENTREPRENEURS—NEW OR ESTABLISHED—HATE TO MAKE COLD CALLS. AND YOU'RE PROBABLY NO EXCEPTION.

So before you make that next call, try these tips:

- Instead of saying "me" and "my company," use words like "you" and "yours." This lets prospects know you're interested in their needs, not just making a sale.
- Practice, practice, practice. To hear how you really sound—and to monitor your use of annoying or distracting phrases—use a tape recorder.
- If you tend to ramble, use a timer. This helps keep you on track and enables you to cover the salient points and not lose your prospect's attention.
- To remind you to smile while you talk, put a mirror next to the phone. Speak in a natural tone, and make sure your enthusiasm for your product or service comes through the phone line.

IN A TIGHT JOB MARKET, IT'S ESSENTIAL THAT ENTREPRENEURS BUILD EMPLOYEE LOYALTY.

Here are some smart ways to build a loyal work force:

- As obvious as it sounds, treat your people well. Create a friendly work environment where communication is frequent and comfortable.
- Employees like to know the results of what they do. When you get feedback from customers, be sure to share that with your staff—the good and the bad.
- Challenge your people. Let your workers try new tasks, perhaps even new jobs within your company. The more challenged employees are, the longer they tend to stay.
- Train your staff. Studies show that employees who received training were more likely to be with their same employer five years later.

ARE YOU
SEEKING
DISTRIBUTION
OUTLETS
FOR YOUR
PRODUCTS?

*Try visiting the stores
you'd like to sell to,
and ask how they buy products.*

You're likely to hear that they
buy from regional buying coopera-
tives or through distributors and
manufacturer's sales reps, or directly from the manufacturer, or from
rack jobbers who put the products
in stores and bill shop owners only
for the merchandise sold.

Once you learn their preferred
method of distribution, call on
those folks to see how they get
their products. Another method is
to read trade magazines aimed at
your market. Call companies selling
new products, explain you're going
to be marketing a new product, and
ask how they distribute theirs.
Make sure you call only noncom-
peting companies—they're usually
more than happy to help new
entrepreneurs.

To make things a little easier, follow these tips the next time you board a plane:

BUSINESS TRAVEL IS RARELY PLEASANT— AND DOING IT DURING THE HOLIDAYS IS ALMOST ALWAYS A NIGHTMARE.

- Use the space above your seat to stow your carry-on bag. If it's full, try to find empty space in front of you so you don't have to go against traffic when the plane lands.
- Try not to block the aisle when stowing your bag. If you're having a problem, let other passengers by before you try again.
- Don't put your heavy suitcase on top of other passengers' coats and jackets. Fold them neatly, and place them on top of your bags.
- Put heavy, breakable or possible leaky items under the seat in front of you, not in the overhead bins.
- If you need assistance from a flight attendant, be polite and patient. At this time of year, they really have their hands full.

It's easy—talk to nearly everyone you meet about your business.

WANT TO KNOW THE SECRET OF NETWORKING?

Think about it this way: If you gave everyone you met in the normal course of your day a business card, a brief introduction to your business and followed up with a short note, you would quickly be able to build awareness of your business. It's easy to find people to pitch your business to. Try these folks:

Bank tellers and loan officers. Neighbors you just happen to run into. Teachers, coaches and other parents you met at your kids' school. Members of your local civic group, chamber of commerce or trade association. The folks who sit next to you on a plane or train. Clerks you meet while shopping. Anyone standing with you in line. People at businesses you frequent. And of course, family and friends.

The key is to look upon everyone you meet as a future client, and keep your company name in front of them.

Is the potential high cost of overhead giving you a headache?

Never fear; there is a low-cost alternative to the high cost of rent. Try leasing space in a shared-office facility or executive business center.

Shared-office facilities offer several options to entrepreneurs seeking space. You can rent space full time or on an as-needed basis. You can choose a tiny cubicle—which costs less, obviously—or a room with a view. And the cost of rent usually includes your space, a phone line, a receptionist, and sometimes furniture.

Most facilities also offer support services on a pay-for-what-you-use basis. These might include secretarial help, use of copy and fax machines, Internet access, computer and graphic services, parking, and use of a conference room.

When considering a facility, check the costs carefully. Make sure the site is convenient and has a reputable business address. Also, is the support staff friendly, is parking convenient, and what's the charge for the furniture, if any?

It's actually smartest to send gifts when customers least expect them.

That way, they appreciate it—and you—more. Before you hit the stores, however, consider these buying tips:

MOST ENTREPRENEURS THINK THE HOLIDAYS ARE THE BEST TIME TO SEND GIFTS TO CUSTOMERS. WELL, THINK AGAIN.

- *Set a budget.* Decide how much money you can spend annually on gifts. The IRS lets you deduct up to $25 for the cost of each business gift.

- *Make a list.* Of course, you'll want to include your best customers. But don't forget those you like best or who are the easiest to deal with. And small gifts are often a good way to land new customers.

- *Choose wisely.* Gifts should enhance your relationships, not detract from them. Don't get too personal. Appeal to your customers' interests.

- *Don't forget to promote your business.* Gifts with your logo, like mugs or clocks, are OK, but only when they're useful and appropriate.

If this sounds like your problem, you need to accelerate income. Here's how:

- Demand deposits upfront.
- Include bills with deliveries, or submit them as soon as you're finished with a job.
- On long-term projects, submit interim invoices.
- Track the payment cycles of your regular clients and customers. Then be sure to bill them in time to be paid in their next cycle.
- Offer discounts for prompt payment or prepayment.
- Don't let past-due accounts slide. Make sure you collect, even if you need to hire a collection service.

FACING A CASH CRUNCH? MOST ENTREPRENEURS DO AT SOME POINT. CASH FLOW PROBLEMS OFTEN STEM FROM SLOW-PAYING CUSTOMERS.

There are other ways to increase your business's income. Consider broadening the scope of your business, adding complementary products or services, or raising prices or fees.

That's a bad strategy.

One of the best ways to let people know you're out there is by sending press releases to a carefully compiled media list.

To get the most from your release, PR maven Alan Caruba says to make sure it contains the following elements:

First, an eye-catching headline that uses action words like "reveals" or "exposes." The lead paragraph should contain a strong quote or statement of general news interest.

In the next paragraph, make sure you state where your company is located and what you do. Then the third paragraph should state the reason for the release. Close strongly, either with a declarative fact or quote. Use a keyword, such as "success," at the start, middle and end of the release.

Finally, make sure the release contains the name and phone and fax numbers of the person to contact for more information. And keep your press release to one page— no one has the time to read more.

NEW ENTREPRENEURS OFTEN DON'T KNOW ENOUGH ABOUT CALLING ATTENTION TO THEIR BUSINESSES, SO THEY DO NOTHING AT ALL.

EVERYBODY WORRIES, BUT NEW ENTREPRENEURS SEEM TO DO MORE THAN THEIR FAIR SHARE.

Worry can paralyze you and can affect the way you respond to clients and employees.

What to do? First, get to the source of your worries. Then take the appropriate action. Many start-up entrepreneurs are overwhelmed by all they have to do and all they haven't done. So it's key to focus and get your mind under control. Try these tips:

- Take it a day at a time, but plan and prioritize what needs to be done tomorrow. Make a list, and check off your accomplishments as you go.
- Estimate how long each task will take you. And be realistic, otherwise you'll get frustrated by trying—and failing—to do too many things at once.
- Unless you are adept at multitasking, try to tackle things one at a time. Move on to the next task only when you have completed the previous one.
- Don't plan every minute. Leave time for the unexpected and the unscheduled.

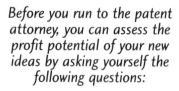

Before you run to the patent attorney, you can assess the profit potential of your new ideas by asking yourself the following questions:

G
GOT A
GOOD IDEA?
NOW WHAT?

- What are the advantages of this idea? Is there a real need for it?
- Do I know exactly what problems my idea will solve?
- Is this an original idea or an adaptation of an existing one?
- What are my anticipated short-term results?
- What are my anticipated long-term gains?
- Are there any faults or limitations to my idea?
- Could this idea create any problems?
- How simple—or complex—will it be to execute this idea?
- Are there variations to this idea? Do I have alternatives?
- Is this idea saleable? Will people want it? Can they afford to pay for it?
- Who is my competition, and what are their plans?

I

INCUBATORS
USUALLY OFFER
A LOW-COST,
NURTURING
ENVIRONMENT
FOR
ENTREPRENEURS
TO NURSE THEIR
FLEDGLING
ENTERPRISES.

*But before you jump
into an incubator, get answers
to these questions:*

- *What is the incubator's mission?*
  Does the management want to
  revitalize a certain area in the
  community, or are they more
  interested in out-of-state or
  international activities?
- *What experiences have other
  tenants had?* Talk to current
  incubator residents as well as
  alumni, and ask their opinions.
- *What is the incubator's track
  record?* How many jobs have
  been created? How many companies have survived once
  they've left?
- *What are its standard operating
  procedures?* Are some services
  free? How long can you stay?
  Will your rent increase as your
  business grows? Does the incubator collect royalties?
- *Do you like the facilities?* Does
  the space meet your needs? Are
  there regular seminars, training
  programs and expert assistance?

MANY BUSY ENTREPRENEURS TRY TO AUGMENT THEIR BUSINESS'S EARNINGS BY INVESTING ONLINE. BUT BE CAREFUL: WEB SCAMS ABOUND.

The Securities Exchange Commission (SEC) offers the following warning tips:

- Investigate before investing. Don't trust what you read. Consult a trusted financial advisor, broker or attorney.
- Check the company out with your state securities regulator and the SEC. Are there complaints?
- Don't assume the offering is what it claims to be or that the backers are who they say they are.
- Ask the online promoter where the firm is incorporated. Verify that information with that state's secretary of state. Is a current annual report on file?
- Get written financial information like a prospectus, annual report or offering circular, and compare them with the online information.
- Be wary of get-rich-quick promises or offers to share "insider" information. Don't trust words like "guarantee," "high return" and "limited offer."

In Growing Up Digital: The Rise of the Net Generation, *author Don Tapscott shares these tips for successfully reaching N-Gen's:*

WANT TO TARGET THE "N GENERATION"? THESE YOUNGER SIBLINGS OF GEN XERS WERE BORN TECH-SAVVY AND SHOULDN'T BE MARKETED TO IN THE SAME OLD WAY.

- *Offer choices.* These kids are exposed to dozens of choices in almost every aspect of their lives. If they can't choose, it's likely you will lose.
- *Let them test-drive it.* N-Gen's like demos. Let them check out what you're selling. The software and game company giants have perfected this. Copy them.
- *Think custom.* This generation is not into mass-marketing. They crave customization. Give it to them.
- *Roll with the changes.* N-Gen's like to change their minds. Blame it on the "with a click of the mouse, you're somewhere else world" of the Internet. So be flexible.
- *Accentuate the functionality.* Don't offer tech for tech's sake. It's not the technology that dazzles this group; rather, they're turned on by function and fun.

IQ353

But membership can be useful.

People tend to do business with people they know—and one of the quickest ways to meet people is through these associations.

Before you sign on, though, make sure the group is worthy of your investment—of dollars and time. Will you get the return you seek? To find out, ask yourself these questions before deciding to join a group:

- What do I want from this group? Advice? Accreditation? Contacts? Friends?
- What do I have to give? Time? Money? Referrals?
- Is the cost greater than the benefits?
- How committed is the group leadership?
- Do I like these people?

Once a member, make sure you spend time at the meetings. And give the group a fair shot—at least a year—before deciding it's not for you.

AMERICANS ARE JOINERS. WE SOMETIMES SIGN UP FOR MORE ORGANIZATIONS, ASSOCIATIONS AND CHAMBERS OF COMMERCE THAN WE HAVE TIME FOR.

ARE YOU A PERFECTIONIST?

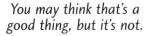

You may think that's a good thing, but it's not.

Entrepreneurs often set impossible standards. Not sure if you're a perfectionist? Take the following test. Do you:

- Get too caught up in details?
- Insist it be done your way?
- Have trouble making decisions and then second-guess yourself once you've finally decided?
- Dwell on what might go wrong?
- Get stressed when things don't go exactly as planned?

If you answered yes to four or more of these questions, you have a problem. Here's how to remedy it:

- *Prioritize:* Focus on what's most important.
- *Be flexible:* Try others' suggestions.
- *Trust:* Let people do what you hired them to do.
- *Don't beat yourself up:* We all make mistakes.

The IRS loves to catch business owners misidentifying employees as independent contractors.

ONE OF THE PROBLEMS THAT PLAGUES ENTREPRENEURS IS THE USE OF INDEPENDENT CONTRACTORS. SURE, IT SOUNDS ENTICING. BUT WAIT— NOT SO FAST.

Independent contractors are self-employed, set their own hours and control their own work. Are you in doubt? The IRS may ask you:

- Is compensation based on hours worked?
- Do you provide the worker with tools and equipment?
- Is the worker free to work for other businesses?
- Must your instructions on how to do the job be followed?
- Is the worker protected from being "fired at will"?

If you answer yes to any of these, you may have an employee on your hands. If you're not sure, check with an attorney, accountant or human resources professional. Even if you are dealing with a true independent contractor, protect yourself with a draft agreement spelling out your relationship.

Don't have a clue how to get a clue? Don't worry; it's easier than you think. Listen up:

WHAT'S HOT? YOU MEAN YOU DON'T KNOW? AS A BUSINESS OWNER, KNOWING WHAT'S HOT AND WHAT'S NOT IS MATTER OF BUSINESS SURVIVAL.

Let your fingers do the walking. Check out the business listings in the Yellow Pages. Which categories are growing? Which are vanishing? Categories crowded with new companies mean opportunity.

Take a stand—a newsstand, that is. Once a month, go to a good-sized newsstand, and check out what's new and what's being featured. Magazines are great indicators of hot consumer markets. For instance, recently launched versions of popular magazines like *Glamour*, *Cosmo* and *People* reflect the growing clout of the Latino market.

Finally, verb it! Keep your ears peeled for nouns being turned into verbs. Usually this signals a rising trend. Words like "access," "network" and "parent" all started out as nouns before they became verbs as well.

Because events often attract attendees with specific profiles and interests, this can be a great way to reach targeted clients and customers.

AS YOUR BUSINESS GROWS, YOU'RE LIKELY TO BE APPROACHED TO SPONSOR SOME TYPE OF INDUSTRY OR COMMUNITY EVENT.

Before you say yes to a sponsorship, first take these steps to protect your investment:

- Examine the event's track record. Look for one that's been around a while and has an established audience. If the event is new, make sure the producer is reputable.
- Get details about expected attendance—how many and who they are.
- Check references. Ask existing sponsors about their experiences.
- Ask if existing sponsorship packages can be customized.
- Look for promotional opportunities. Find out how the event will be marketed, and see if co-op advertising is available.
- Be unique. Will you get industry exclusivity?

Most important, get it in writing. Make sure your agreement is itemized. Have your attorney review the contract to be safe.

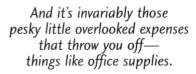

And it's invariably those pesky little overlooked expenses that throw you off— things like office supplies.

Sure, items like pens, pads and tape may seem insignificant, but the costs add up and can have an impact on productivity and profitability. Office superstore Staples offers these tips to help you manage your office-supply expenses better:

YOU PLAN AND YOU BUDGET, BUT SOMEHOW YOU ALWAYS END UP SPENDING MORE THAN YOU THOUGHT.

- Monitor how fast you go through supplies. This will help you know how often to shop and when it's best—and more affordable—to buy in bulk.
- Store supplies where they're accessible and easily trackable. But don't leave them out for everyone to see—and take.
- Even if you prefer to shop in person, use a catalog to compare prices.
- Don't overlook the office-supply store manager. He or she can be a valuable resource who can help you take advantage of the various products and services available.

Do customers and clients enjoy coming to your business?

When people feel good about your business, it's easier for them to trust you and your marketing messages. Here are some simple courtesies that create good will toward you and your business:

DO YOU HAVE A FRIENDLY BUSINESS? PEOPLE ARE MORE AWARE OF YOUR COMPANY'S PERSONALITY THAN YOU MIGHT THINK.

- Set business hours that accommodate a variety of schedules.
- In retail, make sure your merchandise is clearly marked and neatly displayed.
- Remember the names of good customers, and ask how they're doing. You might want to extend special attention to frequent customers.
- Offer a variety of payment options, such as credit cards, installment payments, checks and personal accounts.
- Follow up after the sale to make sure the customer or client is truly satisfied.
- Smile warmly and often. Listen attentively and sincerely say "thank you."

DIRECT MAIL ONLY GENERATES AN AVERAGE **2** PERCENT RESPONSE RATE, SO IT'S VITAL TO DO EVERYTHING YOU CAN TO INCREASE RESPONSE.

Follow these smart tips:

- Start with a list of well-qualified prospects; then test it out—mail 2,500 to 5,000 pieces. And mail to the same list at least two times. Testing should be an ongoing process; you should continually test against your best offer.
- Use a four- or five-component package consisting of an envelope, a letter, a reply card and a return envelope. Inserts are optional. Experts say the more pieces you include, the better. But each piece should explain an additional benefit.
- Remember, the envelope is key. Design yours to reflect what you're selling. And using a teaser on the outside is vital.

For more direct-mail tips, turn the page.

NEED MORE HELP TO INCREASE RESPONSE FROM YOUR DIRECT-MAIL EFFORTS?

Here are four more tips:

- It's best to avoid a monochromatic package. Your envelope and letter can look similar, but use different colors, sizes or textures in the rest of the package.
- Your letter should explain the benefits of your product or service first, then spell out the features. Also, every page of your letter should contain your toll-free number; you never know what part of your package will spur prospects to action.
- Most successful letters include a "Johnson box," a sentence or headline that appears before the salutation. And don't forget the "P.S."—it's the second thing people read, and it should reiterate some aspect of the offer that makes the reader want to know more.
- Your order form should be clear, brief and easy to fill out. Fax numbers increase response.

*Even the smallest staffs
benefit from being charged up.*

Energized employees give you
their best efforts. Here are some
tips to improve your employees'
performance from Bob Nelson,
author of *1001 Ways to Energize
Employees.*

ARE YOUR
EMPLOYEES
ENERGIZED? IF
NOT, THEY
COULD BE
COSTING YOU
MONEY.

- *Involvement:* Involve people in
  decisions that affect their jobs.
  Make sure they know how the
  company works, where it's headed and what their role is.
- *Communication:* Look for creative ways to communicate with
  your staff. Communication is
  more than telling—it's explain-
  ing. Treat people as colleagues,
  not subordinates.
- *Flexibility:* Smart entrepreneurs
  may offer flexibility in where
  employees do their jobs. If flex
  schedules and telecommuting
  can work for your business, give
  them a try. And, in most cases,
  employees will dress appropriately for their situations. No
  dress codes are needed.

IQ363

N

NETWORKING—
EVERYBODY
TALKS ABOUT IT.
BUT DO YOU
KNOW HOW TO
DO IT RIGHT?

*Networking expert
Dee Helfgott says networking
is people connecting with
people—exchanging ideas,
information and resources.
Try her networking tips:*

- *Prepare a 30-second introduction of who you are, what you do and how your business benefits others.* It should be long enough to convey information but short enough so it's not a sales pitch.
- *Volunteer for a small role on a committee of an important organization or association.* This gives you visibility and will gain you respect.
- *Listen more than you talk.* That's the best way to get information that may help you.
- *Don't forget to network outside your group.* You never know who knows someone who may need your product or service.

INTERESTED IN STARTING A BUSINESS ON A BUDGET? WHO ISN'T? AND BOOTSTRAPPING CAN BE ONE OF THE SMARTEST WAYS TO GET STARTED.

Before you do, though, follow these bootstrapping tips:

- Realize some businesses are easier to bootstrap than others. Service businesses, particularly homebased ones, are easier to start up than manufacturing or retail operations.
- If possible, run your business part time at the start. This way, you still have your job income to fall back on, which also allows you to redirect monies back into the company. Again, this favors service entrepreneurs.
- Once you get started, keep your overhead low. If you're a home-based entrepreneur, stay there as long as possible.
- As you try to get your cash flowing, negotiate with vendors and suppliers to get payment extensions.
- Maximize the resources you have. Make do with what you've got until it no longer serves your purpose.

INDEX

SHARE YOUR
TIPS!

As an entrepreneur, I'm sure you've faced your share of problems—and solved them. Share your solutions with us and your fellow entrepreneurs.

Send us your best tips. We may publish them in *Entrepreneur*, *Entrepreneur's Business Start-ups*, our e-zine homeofficemag.com, or in the next edition of this book. If we do, we'll send you a free copy of our booklet *37 Smart Ways to Manage Your Growing Business*.

Send your tips, along with your name, address and phone number to:

> Rieva Lesonsky
> 2392 Morse Ave.
> Irvine, CA 92620,
> or fax us at (714) 755-4211,
> or e-mail us at entmag@entrepreneurmag.com

MILLION DOLLAR

secrets

Exercise your right to make it BIG.
Get into the small business authority
now at 80% off the newsstand price

<u>YES!</u> Start my I year subscription &
bill me for just $9.99. I get a full year of
ENTREPRENEUR & save 80% off the newsstand rate.
If I choose not to subscribe, the free issue is mine to keep.

Name ☐ Mr. ☐ Mrs. _____
(please print)

Address _____

City_____ State _____ Zip _____

[ ] bILL me   [ ] pAymeNt encLOSeD

Guaranteed. Or your money back. Every subscription to Entrepreneur comes with a
100% satisfaction guarantee: your money back whenever you like, for whatever reason, on all
unmailed issues! Offer good in U.S. and possessions only. Please allow 4–6 weeks for mailing of
first issue. Canadian & foreign: $39.97. U.S. funds only.

Mail this coupon to:

5G9J9

Entrepreneur MAGAZINE P.O. Box 50368, Boulder, CO 80321-0368

plus
FREE
issue!